ADVANCED
Fencing Techniques

ADVANCED
Fencing Techniques

Discussions with Bert Bracewell

THE CROWOOD PRESS

First published in 2013 by
The Crowood Press Ltd
Ramsbury, Marlborough
Wiltshire SN8 2HR

www.crowood.com

British Library Cataloguing-in-Publication Data
A catalogue record for this book is available from the British Library.

ISBN 978 1 84797 493 8

Front cover: Senior World Championships, Paris, 2010, Women's Individual Foil final. Elisa Di Francisca (right) and Arianna Errigo (left). (Photo: Graham Morrison)
Back cover: Senior World Championships, Paris, 2010, Men's Individual Sabre final, 2010. Woo Young Won (right), beating Nocolas Limbach (left) for gold. (Photo: Graham Morrison)
Frontispiece: : Leon Paul International, London, 2011, Men's Individual Foil final. Tobia Biono (right) and Husayn Rosowsky (left). Rosowsky won. (Photo: Graham Morrison)

Typeset by Jean Cussons Typesetting, Diss, Norfolk

Printed and bound in Singapore by Craft Print International

Contents

Dedications

Ed: This book is dedicated to my beautiful wife Hilary.

Bert: To my wife Joan, for her love and patience; and for her willingness to leave London for Scotland, where she had never even visited, to give me a chance to follow a career I loved. I have had many successes, but fifty-plus years of marriage is my top achievement!

Acknowledgements

Neil Melville (for his review of *Fencing: Essential Skills Training*); Rebecca Soulen, from Virginia (coaching her at sabre was an introduction to American fencing notation); Michael McCourt (for appearing in photographs); Linlithgow Academy (for permission to photograph on the premises); Edinburgh International Climbing Arena (for permission to photograph on the premises); Sandra Scott, Records Management Officer, The City of Edinburgh Council (for permission to publish the article from *Dolphin*, 1968); Graham Morrison (whose photographs appear on the front and back covers as well as in the book) and Johnstone Syer Photography (photograph of Ed Rogers on the back cover). All other photographs and drawings are by the author.

Also by Ed Rogers

Fencing: Essential Skills Training.

'Sleep with your sword and you will never be lonely.'
'Swordsmanship is next to godliness.'
'Use the sword every day, so that it becomes a part of you.'
Old maxims

'A Master of Arms is more honourable than a Master of Arts, for good fighting came before good writing.'
John Marston, *The Mountebank's Masque,* 1617

Foreword

Bert Bracewell is of that breed of coaches that forms the foundations of fencing throughout the world, providing solid technical training to hundreds of fencers and consistently producing the kind of competitor who inspires respect on the piste. During Bert's reign as National Coach it was very noticeable that the standard of fencing in Scotland rose significantly and Scottish fencers could always be characterized by their very well-rounded technique.

Too many fencers these days are looking for shortcuts and tricks while ignoring the necessity of acquiring a grasp of the fundamentals. This is not only detrimental to the fencer, but in the long term is destructive to the sport itself. Coaches like Bert who have the knowledge and ability to pass on good technique are to be prized.

It has been said, though it takes some courage to say it these days, that fencing belongs to the coaches and is on loan to fencers. It is the coaches who protect and maintain the fundamentals of the sport so that it can continue from generation to generation, and yet they are the ones who stand in the background while the fencer gets the glory. The hard truth is that if a fencer succeeds, then he/she considers himself/herself a remarkably good fencer, but if he/she fails then the coach gets the blame!

The tragedy of fencing is how often the work of the great masters lasts only as long as they are still coaching. Once they hang up their sword, the skills and techniques they have worked so hard to acquire are lost. Throughout the centuries basic techniques and the general philosophy of teaching fencing has generally been handed down by example and/or word of mouth. As a result some techniques have been lost or simply forgotten. I am therefore delighted to be able to commend this book on two fronts – both because it provides a record of Bert's own successful techniques and because Bert himself took such a great interest in the lessons he received or saw from other fencing masters and recorded their techniques, which are reflected here.

These days, any fencer looking for a book on elementary movements and actions is spoilt for choice, but there is very little that goes beyond these. Although many authors have documented, for example, how to execute a disengage, very few have considered and given examples of the vast and varied conditions under which a disengage may be executed. It's refreshing to see that this book begins to address this issue.

In the same way, very little has been written

Professor Philip Bruce.

7

concerning the specifics of the fencing training of competitive fencers generally and even less has been documented concerning the fencing-specific training of fencers competing at the top end of international competitions. For this reason, a book that is written not from a theoretical point of view but based on the thoughts and experiences of a successful fencing master with tried, tested and refined techniques is rare and should prove to be of great value. As the author himself suggests, you may not agree with everything you find, but there is an abundance of ideas and techniques here which any coach or fencer can turn to his or her own use.

One caveat, however – although the sections 'Coaching Formula' and 'Demonstrating to a Class' have many ideas that aspiring coaches may find useful, the reader must remember that this advice is not endorsed by the British Academy of Fencing and there is no substitute for preparing for exams under the supervision of an experienced coach educator who is familiar with the requirements of the particular exam system in question.

Prof. Philip Bruce
President of the British Academy of Fencing

Introduction

I met Bert Bracewell at the school fencing club at Ainslie Park Secondary School, northern Edinburgh, when I was fifteen years old. The club was started by the Head of Physical Education, Finlay McLachlan; it was never part of the school curriculum, just a lunchtime activity. Five times a week we trained and fenced conscientiously. On Fridays, Bert would appear and teach a class. For the rest of the week we practised and fenced; later, some of us became coaches. The club had more than its fair share of success in competitions, particularly in the Scottish Junior and Senior Championships.

Neil Melville, editor of *The Point*, the magazine of Scottish Fencing, wrote the following in a review of *Fencing: Essential Skills Training*:

> Just over thirty-five years ago a remarkable group of young fencers, all from the same school, burst upon the scene. Many of them fenced two or three weapons, but it was the sabreurs whom your reviewer remembers particularly as he was meeting them, successfully or otherwise, on a frequent basis in such events as the Scottish Junior and Senior Championships: youngsters such as Bob Jamieson, George Hanson, Frank Early, Stuart Harrower and Eddie Rogers, all of them noted for their technical skill. Now the last named, himself turned coach, has produced his own book to help fencers – and coaches – improve their skills. Readers of *The Point* may remember a series of articles on sabre training which the author wrote several issues ago… (2005)

Bob, Finlay and I won the Scottish Junior Foil Team Championships back in the late 1960s. Although Finlay was a teacher and we pupils, we shouted at him from the sidelines to improve his game, but made up for this outspoken behaviour by cheering for him when he scored a hit.

Bob went on to become President of Scottish Fencing.

At the Commonwealth Fencing Championships in 1986, it was recognized that Finlay McLachlan had started three out of the five weapon team captains on their fencing careers. In recognition of his coaching achievement, he was awarded the Roger Crosnier Memorial Trophy. He died peacefully in his sleep on 29 July 2010.

I met Bert Bracewell as a teenager and it is fair to say that he left a great impression on me; I expect that I put him on a pedestal. Interestingly enough, even after all these years, the old boy is still on his pedestal.

One of the great factors in competitive fencing is observation of your opponents. Janet Cooksey (previously Wardell-Yerburgh) won the Ladies' Foil at the Commonwealth Games 1970 in Edinburgh. Bert attended as Scottish National Fencing Coach and noticed her placing a chair near the piste. When not fencing, she sat observing her opponents. Watching your opponents can lead to at least one crucial hit in a competition.

In 1970, the Scottish Amateur Fencing Union (SAFU) staged the fencing events at the Commonwealth Games in Edinburgh. This was done with such efficiency that Gold Medals of the Amateur Fencing Association (AFA) were awarded to Dr L.G. Morrison and J.L. (Tommy) Hope, respectively President and Secretary of SAFU. The award of merit, inaugurated in 1969, was conferred on Christine Tolland, especially for her organization of the games. Tommy Hope, a Scottish Champion a total of nine times at all weapons, had been drawn into administration, when he succeeded his brother Arthur as Secretary of the Scottish Fencing Club in 1929. They were also kinsmen to Sir William Hope, the distinguished

Scottish fencing master, celebrated swordsman, deputy-governor of Edinburgh Castle and fencing writer. His whose greatest work, *A New Short and Easy Method of Fencing or the Art of the Broad and Small-Sword*, was printed in Edinburgh in 1707: a list of his published works is included in the Bibliography of Egerton Castle's *Schools and Master of Fence*, originally published in 1885. Sir William Hope was also the founder of the Society of Sword Men in Scotland.

When talking with foreign coaches, Bert asked, 'What is wrong with British fencing?' He expected answers like, 'Not good enough' or 'Not fit', but the response he got was, 'They don't know where the point is' (at foil and épée). A good fencer will know where the point is at all times, and this will come through lengthy training and years of experience.

Even the best fencers can become unsettled, fencing wilder and wilder. Bert knew an Italian coach who would shout 'box' during a fight if his fencer's technique became unruly. The fencer was then required to come on guard perfectly, fencing neatly within an imaginary box, with all positions careful and precise and always perfectly balanced.

Bert tells a story about his coach, Alf Simmonds. He had taken a lesson which cost him seven shillings and six pence, a lot of money in those days. Afterwards, Alf took him outside and showed him a storm drain. He explained that he had given him exactly the same lesson the week before and, because he had not bothered to practise, he had ended up giving him the same lesson again. He suggested jokingly that if Bert was not going to practise, he might as well throw his money down the drain. Practice makes perfect.

It is not enough to be faster than your opponents. There are three types of speed: point, arm and leg. If the arm is already straight, then speed comes from the legs. In a riposting situation arm and point speeds combine. A slightly bent arm at the beginning of an attack can get the point travelling faster. When technique is equal between two opponents, they revert to speed. When speed is equal, they revert back to technique.

Mere speed does not always ensure the success of an attack. A very fast compound attack against an opponent with a slow parry may result in an opponent parrying himself. In this case, speed should be reduced to allow the defender time to form the parry. The correct cadence in such cases is a speed just a little faster than that of one's opponent.

Bert observed that many continental coaches are 'developing masters' and felt that most British coaches were 'corrective masters'. Due to time constraints, say one lesson a week, faults build up – perhaps through competition, change of weapon, etc. The coach will spend much of the time correcting these. Bert rarely had time to spend developing a fencer. One notable exception to this was Michael Breckin, whom he used to give three to four lessons a week. Bert was only part qualified at the time and Michael would be waiting for him on his doorstep when he got home from work. The lessons were given in the lounge but, judging from the red marks on the ceiling from the foil tips, some may not have gone entirely as planned. When fencing for England in the 1970 Commonwealth Games, Michael won gold medals in the individual foil and foil team when Bert was Scottish National Coach. Scottish fencers also won an impressive five medals. That same year, Bert himself won the Men's Foil title at the Inverclyde Open Tournament. It is not the fault of British masters that they do not have the time or venues to coach like this.

It may seem a bit eccentric giving fencing lessons in your lounge. I called an old friend, whom I had not spoken to for some time, and interrupted him giving an épée lesson in his kitchen. Fencing is a sport which attracts people who are mildly eccentric. Consider the case of Geoff King of Latista Fencing Club. He drove an old open-topped Rolls Royce and had lost the sight of one eye in an air crash. One day he gave Bert a lift. He wore a tight-fitting, close-necked black sweater over his white, high-necked fencing jacket. They stopped at some road works. The policeman supervising said, 'Come on through, vicar.' Geoff was a good coach and fencer.

In an individual lesson you get exercise, correct training and confidence. Because you learn the extremities of what is possible, you will do a wider range of strokes when you fence competitively. The cheapest way of learning to fence is to take four lessons a week, because this gives you the best return.

The idea for this book came when Bert found some old notes while clearing out his loft. He used to keep a record of fencing lessons with other masters, and then discuss them with his coach, whose reaction would be to accept or reject, but always to understand why. There was nothing wrong in any advanced fencing techniques, only variations, which he had learned from other masters or through observations in his long career. Many became fashionable at different times, but the real interest was in exploring fencing strokes in depth.

Are we training people to become swordsmen, to learn about the techniques of fencing, or to simply win competitions? Often these days it is simply about winning competitions.

Bert tells a story about the use of (the parry) prime. For ten years he had not seen prime used at foil, nor been trained to use it. The classical foil masters did not teach it, and then prime was rediscovered. Just before he came to Scotland in 1966, its use in foil became widespread. On a fencing course run by Bob Anderson, Bert asked about the use of prime. Bob Anderson thought the use of prime fine, but in his position he dare not teach it as many of his coaches might use it indiscriminately, simply because it was fashionable. In 1949, the AFA, thanks to the foresight of their Secretary, C-L. (Charles) de Beaumont, appointed the French Olympic Coach, Roger Crosnier, as National Coach. Part of Crosnier's contract was to train his successor and he chose Bob Anderson to train both competitively and in the skills of training fencing teachers and coaches. In 1953, Bob Anderson succeeded Roger Crosnier as National Coach to Great Britain and Northern Ireland.

Fencing strokes become fashionable, much as our clothes change fashion. In the eighteenth century, the rapier became too heavy and cumbersome to wear in polite society. The sword steadily lightened in weight to become the court sword, which had a much shorter blade. This lighter weapon could be used with significantly more skill and precision, using the fingers to manipulate the sword. The French school of fencing had begun.

In his time, Bert has seen the transformation of national competitions from 'steam' to electric foil. He was first introduced to electric foil when his club Latista made the last four in the British Team Foil Championships. The preliminary rounds were fenced as before, but in the final they were informed that remaining bouts would be fenced using the new electric foil equipment. They were loaned electric kit, but had no idea how to use it effectively. Salle Paul won by attacking in the low-line, prompting Alf Simmonds to purchase one of the new rudimentarily designed electric boxes. Simmonds had studied with Roger Crosnier and had received lessons, at different times, from many accomplished masters, including Bob Anderson and Bill Harmer-Brown. He was also distinguished in his day, having been the youngest RSM in the Coldstream Guards.

From then on, Bert became interested in coaching, watching and receiving many lessons. Over the course of his long career, he has studied many advanced fencing techniques, but never before has he taught this vast array of knowledge to any one person. To understand this required over two and a half years of special one-to-one lessons and discussions at Wallace Fencing Club, in order to perform each action correctly, record it, and write this book. What follows is a testimony to the remarkable ability and memory of a man in his seventies, as well as the unique relationship that can exist between master and pupil.

These techniques come from a variety of sources. Any master can become a good coach, but only exposure to other masters makes a master possible. In this sense, one master is made up of many others; each added to the art of fencing as we know it today. Fencers are driven to win and likely to concentrate on those aspects which help them succeed. *Advanced Fencing Techniques* will not only help the aspiring fencer improve, but also the established fencer who may be looking for new ideas. Equipment and rule changes over the years have shown fencers that they must adapt with the times. Tried and tested approaches have often been challenged as a result. *Advanced Fencing Techniques* offers a unique collection which can be used to develop new fencers, as well as providing a repository of knowledge for the future.

In the descriptions that follow, the actions will be carried out by two right-handed fencers, unless otherwise mentioned. I should add also that the use of the masculine 'his' is simply a writing convention, not a chauvinistic tendency on my behalf. There are many fine women fencers for whom this book will be equally relevant and for whom I have the greatest possible respect.

For readers in the United States and others who are used to numerical terminology like 'fourth' and 'one', instead of 'quarte' and 'prime', I would ask you to bear with me. I have read some excellent publications that use numerical notation and found that this did not spoil my enjoyment.

Similarly, I hope that readers experiencing typical British terminology will not be put off.

From a historical standpoint it is important that these advanced fencing techniques are recorded. Many very successful fencing masters have left no records of their teachings, other than in the memories and acquired skills of their pupils. This detailed record takes the reader through a step-by-step series of discoveries, where familiar topics are introduced then developed in numerous, often diverse ways and rediscovered, leading to an understanding of the techniques required to become an advanced fencer or an advanced coach.

Feel free to accept, or reject – but at least understand why.

PART I

Advanced Fencing Techniques

1 Foil

An examination of advanced fencing techniques is essentially about studying variations within set themes. These have been passed on over generations by many excellent fencing masters, who taught different things and believed in what they did. They include the classical French style as espoused in the writings of Roger Crosnier, whose three main books are *Fencing with the Foil*, *Fencing with the Sabre* and *Fencing with the Épée*. He also wrote *Fencing with the Electric Foil*, in

ON PREVIOUS PAGE: Fig. 1 'A' Grade, at Crystal Palace, London, 2011, Women's Team Sabre. Ni Hong (China), left, and Svetlana Kormilitsyna (Russia), right. (Photo: Graham Morrison)

LEFT: Fig. 2 Eden Cup, Men's Individual Foil Semifinal, 2010. Race Imboden (USA), left, and Alexander Choupenitch (Czech Republic), right. (Photo: Graham Morrison)

which he studied the use of the then new Electrical Registering Apparatus for foil. Épée had been electrified in the 1930s and it was only a matter of time before the same happened to foil. Electric foil was first used in a major event at the 1955 World Championships in Rome. This marked the end of traditional academic foil play – light, stylish, and with complexity – which had not materially altered since the introduction of the wire mask in the late eighteenth century. Top-ranking fencers lacked experience using the new top-heavy blades, which caused the sword hand to move slower; blade play became risky. Hits to the low-line, previously hidden to the judges by the sword arm, began to register. During these bouts, simple movements predominated; fencing phrases became shorter, with increasing use of absence of blade. Feint attacks were less frequent because of the popularity of counter-attacks, as foil, in some respects, began to resemble épée. Rather than counter-riposte, to remise offered more chances of success.

All this required a radical rethink.

There was a Scottish dimension to Roger Crosnier's early life. In 1909, the Scottish Fencing Club was formed in Edinburgh, with Professor Leon Crosnier as its fencing master, assisted in due course by his eldest son Roger, who spent long hours training under his father's tutelage.

It is hard for us to imagine today what a fencing tournament was like before the advent of electrical scoring apparatus. With four judges and a president (which is what a referee was called in those days) per piste, there could be a lot of talking going on around you while you fenced. In those gentlemanly days, if a fencer stopped fencing and was hit, he could ask for the hit to be annulled, claiming that he had stopped in good faith mistakenly responding to a president on another piste.

In the topics which follow we will begin with a basic understanding of each stroke and then take it to a more advanced level.

The Grip

With a French grip the foil is carried between thumb and forefinger, with the other three fingers placed lightly against the handle. Pushing with the thumb and pulling with the forefinger makes the point dip; this process, carried out in reverse, brings the point up again. The pommel should be maintained on an axis parallel to the forearm. The French grip is proportioned, so that its convex curve lies across the palm of the hand.

Straight Thrust Simple Attack

As beginners, we first learn the importance of simple attacks, which are by definition single blade movements. These can be direct or indirect. The only direct simple attack is the straight thrust. The three indirect simple attacks are the disengagement, cutover and counter-disengagement. To the advanced foil fencer a simple attack can be a championship-winning stroke.

A simple attack can be made to the high- or low-line, or the side of the target. If an opponent ducks down to avoid being hit, it can even revert to the back. Simple attacks can be made into blade, or into footwork preparations.

Preparations may be compound if two or more preparations are made continuously without a pause. A typical compound preparation might be to step forward and engage your opponent's blade, the engagement coinciding with the landing of the attacker's rear foot; the actions are made in the same period of fencing time, with the foot and hand working together. Double preparations follow each other, with a pause in between: for example, the blade is engaged, then a beat attack is launched, after a slight pause. If preparations are complex, then the finish should be simple, otherwise the chance of error creeps in.

To begin to understand how an advanced fencer thinks, we must understand the difference between opportunistic and creative actions. Generally speaking, the expression 'actions' refers to blade movements – offensive or defensive. Opportunistic actions rely on your opponent making mistakes. Creative actions are more important since the attacker initiates what will happen next. Faced with the challenge of producing an all-important winning hit, a creative action will serve you best.

An attacker must prepare the way. Imagine

a situation where the attacker first presents the blade. The point may be extended, towards the eyes, immediately getting the defender's attention; now launch any attack.

Consider the following:

1. The fencers begin at lunge distance to body. The defender simply takes the blade away, offering an open target. The attacker sees this opportunity and lunges with a straight thrust to target (*see* Fig. 3). In a fencing bout this would never happen; few opponents are so helpful as to simply give a hit away. This technique has limited value in teaching tactical fencing to more advanced students. An improving fencer would be looking for a means to create a hit, using his own initiative.

2. Next, the attacker first applies pressure on the opponent's blade to create an opening for a straight thrust with detachment (*see* Fig. 4). It is sufficient to make light contact, pressing the defender's blade out of line with a rapid firm action. The pressure is applied at the middle of the opponent's blade by closing the last three fingers of the sword hand and slightly flexing the wrist. Attacks with pressure tend to be successful when the opponent does not respond immediately, perhaps waiting to see

ABOVE: Fig. 3 An opportunistic opening from absence of blade.

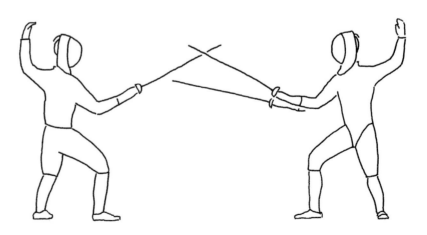

RIGHT: Fig. 4 Pressure is applied to the opponent's blade to create an opening.

what may develop. A heavy pressure might make the defender respond instinctively, laterally, possibly requiring the attacker's disengagement. If the attacker applies a pressure, the defender might respond by rotating the blade through circular sixte, requiring the attacker to do a counter-disengagement – a more difficult stroke, brought about by the more advanced fencer changing the line. The attacker has created an opening by taking the initiative, but the use of detachment in concluding the hit may allow your opponent's hit to land also, requiring a decision from the referee.

3. This time the attacker applies pressure on the defender's blade and follows this with a straight thrust with opposition. Holding onto the blade removes the possibility of the other side's hit landing. This is a stroke more typical at épée, but effective at foil nevertheless.

These exercises can be performed from sixte and quarte. Attacks must be made 'in time' and at the correct distance.

Joseph Vince refers to two types of timing in *Fencing*: conscious and subconscious. Conscious timing is where the tempo is chosen when the opponent is in motion. The opponent may be doing any of a number of things unconsciously: rising, or sinking, in the on guard position; advancing, retreating, or recovering from a lunge; making a feint, or a beat, without the intention of attacking; engaging or disengaging the blade; moving from one guard position to another (invitation). Subconscious timing is when a fencer chooses a moment to attack, suggested by instinct.

Generally speaking, attacks are carried out after adequate preparations, surprising the defender and using the attacker's tempo. They should be fast, unlikely to be detected in advance, taking advantage of the opponent's shortcomings through careful observation.

One-Two Compound Attack
Compound attacks consist of a number of simple attacks, one or more being used as a feint. A feint is a false attack which your opponent thinks is real

and reacts to; you are exploiting his instinctive reactions. A one-two compound attack is a feint of a disengagement followed by a second disengagement. Every compound attack is an example of second intention.

Occasionally, I have heard Bert refer to composed attacks (the feints are composed), which, in the French school, are compound attacks, as previously described. However, William Gaugler in *A Dictionary of Universally Used Fencing Terminology*, reminds us that, in Italian fencing theory, compound or composed attacks can be divided into three groups: feints, actions on the blade and renewed attacks. With regard to sabre, Julio Martinez Castello in *The Theory and Practice of Fencing* describes compound attacks which may be preceded by attacks on the blade. Composed parries consist of two or more successive parries. Waneen Wyrick in *Foil Fencing* describes successive parries as compound parries. With sabre, Michel Alaux in *Modern Fencing: Foil, Épée, and Sabre* describes successive parries as combination parries. These consist of different hand positions, at a slow pace, which are not necessarily reactions to feints but a means of closing a line, subtly directing the attack into a line that will be blocked by the final parry. This may be thought of as an offensive–defensive action. Regardless of which term you wish to use for successive parries, general wisdom seems to suggest that to be effective at foil and épée, the types of parry should alter each time: a lateral parry may be followed by a circular one, a diagonal parry by a circular one, and so on. When you find yourself following the attacker's blade, you are usually at least one motion behind. Retreating with the first parry, this should be perfectly placed, and may provide a little extra time in which to position the second.

Once again we will consider the difference between opportunistic and creative actions.

1. Begin at lunge distance to body. The defender goes for the blade. The attacker seizes on this opportunity and launches a one-two. The defender reacts to the feint of disengagement with a lateral parry, allowing the attacker a second disengagement, which

is completed with a lunge. The attacker is simply waiting for an opportunity from an extremely obliging opponent to present itself.

2. The next example, although still opportunistic, is slightly more difficult. The defender moves a little further away. This time he does a sharp move very close to the blade, then goes for it. This instantly changes the timing of the attacker's one-two, forcing him to react; but this opportunity is still being provided by the defender. For best effect, this can be practised very quickly following the previous exercise: the defender goes for the blade and the attacker launches the one-two; quickly, he moves very close to the blade, drawing out the distance and goes for it again, getting a quick reaction from the one-two and instantly changing the timing.

3. Now the timing will be controlled more creatively by the attacker. The attacker stands on guard in octave, or with the blade held parallel to the floor, and lifts the blade up when ready. The attacker switches on his brain in response to this action and becomes alert. This provides the defender with an opportunity to go for the blade and the one-two is launched as before. A fencer might meet an opponent who likes to go for the blade. He might present the blade with brief lifting actions, trying to get a reaction. A short pause after the lift might draw the necessary response. To do this it is likely that he will have observed the opponent's fencing earlier and decided on a possible course of action. Observation of your opponent is crucial to the success of strokes like this.

4. In the classical tradition fencers would begin with blades engaged in sixte. Traditionally they would fence with the front foot lining up with the toe of the opponent's rear foot, which created a certain dynamic, since only one fencer could be covered. Modern fencers, however, compete toe-to-toe and if the blades are engaged both are covered. The attacker begins by applying pressure to the blade to open the line. The defender responds, attempting to cover. The attacker replies with a feint of disengagement, drawing a parry of quarte, followed by a second disengagement. However, modern fencers do not fence from positions of engagement, preferring absence of blade; also, an experienced fencer will not attempt to parry a feint that far away, preferring to parry at the last possible moment, when the point is much closer to the target and the attacker more vulnerable to a sudden riposte. This leaves us with the problem of how to do a one-two against a defender who does a very effective late parry.

In the traditional Italian and German schools, 'engagement' meant domination of the opposing blade: strong, or middle, against weak. For the traditional French and English, as here, this implies only blade contact.

5. The straight thrust with disengagement in mid-lunge is probably the most commonly used one-two attack in modern fencing (*see* Fig. 5). If you attack with a straight thrust your point might hit, be parried, or your opponent might step back. In the event of a parry, with an opponent who parries late effectively, the attacker's last action will need to be taken while the foot is still in mid-air. A good way of training to do this is to start with a straight thrust, which must land correctly. The defender then introduces an occasional late parry, which should be deceived in mid-lunge, but not every time. If there is no parry then the straight thrust should always land, otherwise the one-two would be self-defeating. I have referred to this as a one-two, but a purist would disagree, since this does not start with disengagement.

1 to 5 can be practised at fixed distance, or preceded by steps forward or backward to add mobility.

To the advanced fencer a better understanding of the types of one-two is essential to developing

Fig. 5 A straight thrust with disengagement in mid-lunge.

a more versatile game. In the examples that follow we will consider different techniques:

6. Consider the drifting feint. This starts close to the blade, the point/hand drifting out, eliminating the possibility of a circular parry of sixte. The feint begins slowly, suddenly drifting out to induce the wider parry of quarte, giving more time for the attacker to complete the one-two. This is useful against an opponent who has a well-formed parry of circular sixte and is perhaps less confident with, or is prone to, an exaggerated parry of quarte.

7. In the 'swallowtail' one-two, the attacker begins by applying pressure to the defender's blade. The defender returns this pressure, giving the attacker an opportunity for disengagement with a feint, which could easily be parried by a short parry of quarte. Then the hand moves across 6 inches (150mm), angulating the point in to draw a wider, more exaggerated parry of quarte, similar to the drifting feint earlier. The attacker finishes by angulating the same amount on the other side after the disengagement – making the defender's return journey from an exaggerated quarte, to sixte, even more difficult. The angulated positions of the feint and the disengagement, prior to the lunge, result in the 'swallowtail' description.

Angulating the wrist makes it difficult for the opponent to form an effective parry. All types of attacks and counter-attacks may be delivered this way. The advantage of hitting with the point, at an angle near 90 degrees to the target, is that it is less likely to slip off. The disadvantage, at sabre and épée, is that of exposing the arm; here, angulation should be left to the last possible moment.

8. Disengagement is a narrow 'V'-shaped up-and-down action. A one-two consisting of two disengagements is a tight 'V'-shaped formation. An alternative to this is the wider 'U' shape, which can also cause a more exaggerated parry of quarte. The 'U' starts with the attacker's point drifting out. The defender's eye follows the feint, accompanied by his hand reacting to quarte. It is necessary for the attacker's hand to move faster in the second part of the 'U' in order to avoid an effective defence of successive parries, quarte-sixte. However, a slow 'U'-shaped one-two might be done to initiate successive parries of quarte-sixte deliberately, thus leaving the defender vulnerable to a finish in the low-line.

9. A straight thrust with disengagement in mid-lunge is launched against an unsuspecting opponent, but this time the final action is angled at the last moment to avoid hitting

Fig. 6 The feint begins with a slightly bent arm...

the off-target sword arm. Competitive foil-ists tend to cover their targets. Some will duck down as they lunge forward, making it harder to hit the valid target.

10. If a fencer has a fine classical quarte parry, the attacker's point can drop 3 inches (75mm) with the feint, inducing either a bad parry of quarte or quinte. Lowering the parry of quarte is a common fault. A trained fencer, looking to parry the blade forte to foible, may simply react by drifting low. As the point is only beginning to move into the low-line, a sudden parry of septime may not immediately suggest itself.

11. A one-two where the point is dropped under the guard on the feint allows the parry of quarte to pass over. Dropping the point places the attacker's blade at a similar angle to the defender's. If the defender's parry of quarte is taken correctly, the blade will pass over. The attacker simply lifts the point to continue with the second movement of the attack.

12. The feint can be presented with a slightly bent arm, which has the effect of accelerating the second action: slow start, quick finish (*see* Figs 6–7). The hand has to accelerate to catch up with the foot. If the point hits at a slight angle, this can speed up the 'bite'

Fig. 7 ...which has the effect of accelerating the second action.

of the hit, which should still hit with the character of penetration. At the advanced level a fencer would have to be given a reason for responding to a bent arm feint. One way would be to perform the feint progressively, making the second disengagement with the foot in mid-air even more devastating. This should not be confused with the broken time one-two, where the foot is allowed to land before the hit is made.

13. A broken time one-two can be used against an opponent who either parries late or takes successive wide parries. The attacker lunges with a deep feint, pulling his hand back to avoid the parry as the front foot lands, then straightens the arm to complete the one-two (*see* Fig. 8). Broken time is unconventional; it goes against the flow of the fight, abruptly interrupting the normal expectations of the defender. A successful conclusion requires a considerable element of surprise.

Broken time is useful against a defender who parries late, or parries wildly with successive parries, trying to find the blade. An attack may be delivered in two-time, with a pause in the middle, or there may be a pause before the final action of a compound riposte. Useful at foil and sabre, broken time tends to be accidental at épée.

Another variation to this might be when the attacker disengages, then suddenly withdraws the sword arm, launching the second disengage, with lunge, from the bent arm position.

Charles Simonian, in *Get the Point! A Fencer's Handbook*, refers to what he terms a 'modern disengage attack'. The feint is made in the usual way, but the extended arm is flexed to deceive the parry, then re-extended immediately to hit into the newly opened line. This technique can be used against lateral or circular parries and the withdrawal held back if successive parries are to be deceived.

14. The final action of the one-two can be performed with opposition, closing the line at the end. This responds to a fencer who simply counter-attacks. Épéeists fencing foil may do this, as their natural reaction is to counter-attack.

All of the above can be performed from sixte and quarte and revert to the low-line.

Here, there is much to choose from. In a day at a fencing competition, a fencer will fence many times. As he approaches the later stages of a competition, it will be clear to his opponents what his best strokes are. These are the ones the fencer likes to do because he has learned that they give the best results. An advanced fencer will observe his weaknesses, dig deep and change his game.

Next, we shall consider defence.

Fig. 8   A broken time one-two.

Economic Parry of Quarte

The hand position of the economic parry of quarte tends to be the classical French style, as taught by Roger Crosnier: the hand is kept in the half-supinated position. In America there is a wide variety of approaches to quarte, which they call the fourth parry: Paul Sise, in *A Basic Foil Companion*, shows fourth taken with the hand in supination (2 o'clock) and then with the hand towards pronation (11 o'clock); Muriel Bower, in *Foil Fencing*, describes the thumb position in four as 1 o'clock; Jules Campos, in *The Art of Fencing*, describes the fourth parry taken with the thumb on top (which I take to mean 12 o'clock), as shown in Fig. 9; and Nancy L. Curry, in *The Fencing Book*, describes the sixth position starting at 1 o'clock and fourth at 11 o'clock. Thomas Cross and Ernie Kirkham in *Introduction to Fencing* describe the sixth parry as 2 o'clock and the fourth as 12 o'clock.

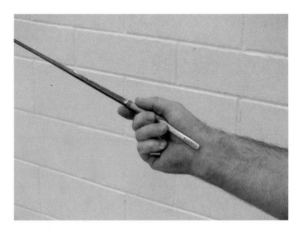

Fig. 10　The fourth parry – 1 o'clock.

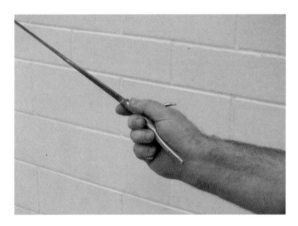

Fig. 9　The fourth parry – 12 o'clock.

Begin in sixte with the hand in half-supination – that is, the thumb rotated to 1 o'clock (*see* Fig. 10). If the master places a foil parallel to the floor, under and next to the guard, quarte can be practised by moving in a straight line along this axis, without turning the hand. The master's guard can be positioned where the parry is to be formed. Alternatively, the foil can be placed separately, touching the side of the body; when the blade is just lifted away, this is the position of the parry. The parry of quarte will be naturally wider in a fight, because the fencer is under pressure.

Some masters advocate the use of quinte as a replacement for quarte, believing it to be more effective. In this book, however, quinte is a distinctly different parry and can take either of two forms: one at normal height and the other a little lower. I can well understand why masters would choose to teach this as an effective foil parry as it keeps the point clear of the off-target sword arm, leading to a riposte on the side and back that is difficult to parry. For those who advocate a full-supinated riposte from quarte taken in the 3 o'clock position (*see* Fig. 11), the riposte will

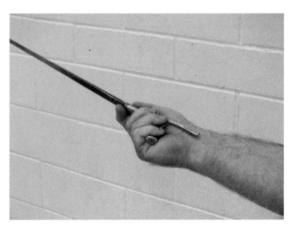

Fig. 11　The fourth parry – 3 o'clock.

clear the mask, even if the opponent lunges close and ducks down. Interestingly, holding the guard in the centre of the valid target and turning the hand half a turn to the right and left, to parry sixte and quarte, is still an extremely effective defence at foil and épée.

If a fencer does not respond to any particular system, for physical reasons perhaps, you can adapt the hand positions accordingly. Actually, it does not matter what system you follow, providing you attend enough lessons and follow the advice of your coach.

Parries on the Left Side

A parry like quarte is the bread and butter of fencing. Based on instinctive movements it is easy to learn, but successful execution requires good judgement. What follows was originally taught to me under the term 'fourteen parries of quarte', but this title has been changed as the hand movements described here can vary between quarte and quinte.

1. When new fencers have problems parrying quarte, i.e. the point goes way out to the left, they can be taught the 'bridge' parry. Starting in sixte, the hand takes a slight curving action, as if crossing a small imaginary bridge. This is a useful way of correcting the parry of quarte in younger fencers. Over-reacting on the quarte side is an instinctive reaction with inexperienced fencers.

2. The classical riposte from quarte is with half-supination. The parry is taken in the 1 o'clock position and the hand turns to the 3 o'clock position with the riposte. This drags the point clear of the mask, when the attacker is lunging forward, hard. The parry of quarte is taken in the usual way with the wrist broken. The wrist is then rotated during the riposte, so that the hand is in supination: useful against an opponent who ducks down, trying to cover the target with his mask.

We tend to take the use of the mask in modern fencing a little for granted. Félix Gravé, in *Fencing Comprehensive*, illustrates the evolution of

the mask and attributes Texier La Boëssière as conceiving a mask made of wire in 1760, allowing fencers to move faster and with greater safety.

3. Next, the classical parry of the line of quinte can be used, which pushes the attacker's point down, leaving a little more time for a direct riposte with detachment. Quinte is the fifth parry, or guard position, defending the inside high-line (*see* Fig. 12). A more typical riposte from quinte would be to the side or back, which has the advantage of avoiding the unarmed sword arm (*see* Figs. 13–14).

Fig. 12   Quinte, the fifth parry, or guard position.

H.A. Colmore Dunn, in *Fencing*, refers to the alternative name for quinte as low quarte, which is intended to protect the debatable ground between the line of quarte and septime, being lower than one and higher than the other. He stipulates that quinte may be formed with the hand in pronation or supination.

4. The riposte from quarte can be done with opposition. This is used a lot at épée and removes the possibility of the attacker's remise. Traditionally, a remise would be used against a fencer who parries incompletely, delays the riposte, or uses an indirect or compound riposte.

Fig. 13   Quinte.

Fig. 14   Riposte to
the low-line.

5. The defender comes on guard with his sword arm in a central position. The parry is formed by rolling the wrist, until the blades make contact. This makes for a very short parry and a fast riposte. Much, however, depends on the referee's interpretation as to whether or not the point has been cleared from the defender's target. In the early part of the last century, if the blades touched, this was considered to be a parry. When playing to a classical referee this could be a winning stroke. Sixte can also be parried from this position.

6. The next parry is taken bearing down onto the blade, with the riposte in opposition to the back or flank. The hand is turned a little towards quinte, which is helpful against a taller opponent. This was demonstrated to me and was extremely effective.

7. Another parry is taken bearing down onto the blade and riposting with opposition. As the blade drops, the rear foot goes out to the right, which allows more room to hit the opponent's target. This is particularly useful against an attacker who has done a flèche and may be temporarily off the piste.

8. The lifting parry of quarte, taken with the hand high, lifts the point and opens up an opportunity for a riposte to shoulder, or back against a low attack, changing the angle of the riposte.

9. The dropping parry of quarte, taken with the hand low, is particularly useful against a flèche because it takes the attacker's point down, stopping the flèche attack from landing. Lifting and dropping parries, which are Hungarian in origin, both change the angle of the riposte.

10. The traditional beat-parry is delivered in the centre of the blade: essentially a beat, taken defensively into the attacker's preparation. This short–sharp action deflects the attacker's point and gets the hand moving forward straightaway into the riposte. It is very effective when fencing with the front feet toe to toe, as in the modern game.

Aldo Nadi in *On Fencing* describes two ways to parry: by holding the blade briefly, but firmly, in the exact parry position; and by spanking the opponent's blade out powerfully, as above. In a holding parry, the adversary's blade will slide along your own – typically, parries and combinations of parries ending in sixte and seconde. Parries and combinations of parries ending in quarte or septime may be learned both ways.

In *The Art of the Foil*, Luigi Barbasetti describes a form of simple parry, which he calls a 'tap' or 'slinging parry'. He suggests that a tap parry can only be carried out against a definite thrust, never against a feint. This type of parry is distinguished by a much greater movement of the point, exceeding the limits set by simple parries. The tap parry is made with the centre of your blade against the centre of your opponent's, essentially a beat.

Both of the above refer to observations in the use of Italian foils. Bac H. Tau (of the French school), in *Fencing: Volume One, Competitive Training and Practice*, calls this a tac parry.

11. The rolling-hand parry of quarte and riposte is very fast: rotating the wrist from sixte, with the thumb at 1 o'clock, to quarte at 11 o'clock. Riposte immediately on contact with the blade. Once again we find ourselves in the hands of the referee, who must determine if the attacker's point has been cleared from the defender's target.

12. The Italian rolling parry to the left may end up in quarte, halfway between quarte and quinte, or quinte. This is useful if, as in traditional Italian foil, the weapon is strapped to the wrist. Continuation of the rolling hand leads to an effective riposte with opposition, with strong possession of the blade.

13. This time the parry of quarte is taken in supination, with the thumb at 3 o'clock. A detached low-line riposte is easy from this position, as the supinated hand drops between high and low with relative ease.

14. Deliberately parry quarte with the point out and the blade angled at about 40 degrees. The riposte is to low-line, or back, with opposition. Some modern Hungarian-

trained coaches parry quarte without break-ing the wrist, which leads to a similar hand position. They argue that this makes for a stronger parry; but if the parry is taken correctly, with the wrist broken and the forte of the defender's blade against the foible of the attacker's blade, there should be little chance of the attack getting through.

These are the fourteen parries as they were taught to me.

The advanced fencer is always open to new ideas, or more likely old ones which have been recycled, if they work. He will try to set up the right conditions for a particular stroke to prepare the way. For example, one of the most common blade preparations is the beat attack, which we will tackle next.

Beat Attacks

C-L. de Beaumont in *Your Book of Fencing* describes the beat being made by opening the last three fingers of the sword hand, closing them again with a slight flexing of the wrist, to deliver a sharp blow on the opponent's blade. The oppos-ing blade is struck, by bringing the handle smartly back to its original position. The strength of the beat may vary. A strong beat can be used to create an opening, a light beat, used passively, to induce a reaction, or vice versa. This is not to be confused with the pressure, which like the beat is applied in the middle of the opponent's blade, but is more subtle. Beginners sometimes extend the arm while beating, which should be avoided, as the beat will land too far down the blade. A good beat should be delivered with an element of surprise, not used repeatedly.

What follows next are six classical ways of learning a beat attack.

1. First, two pieces of tape are applied to the centre of the defender's blade, with a gap in the middle. The attacker then practises the beat methodically on the correct part of the blade. Slow repetition of the beat, followed by arm extension as a continuous fluid action, is what is required. Gradually the fencer learns

to make the beat in the correct place with crisp precision.

2. A fencer can do a very hard beat, followed quickly by a light beat, to which his experi-enced opponent does not react. The oppo-nent's mind and hand become attuned to the heavy beat, allowing the light beat to slip through. A beat can seek out a reaction, or the lack of it. To think of a beat as a probing action leads to a better understanding of what may happen next. A beat that is obvious and slow may lead to a disengagement by the defender, requiring the attacker to think about taking a parry and the possible use of second intention. An advanced fencer might opt to do a slow beat deliberately, in order to draw a disen-gagement from an opponent who is prone to attacking on the preparation. If stepping forward with the beat, the step might be delib-erately foreshortened to allow time to parry and riposte.

3. Alternatively, a light beat can be followed by a hard beat. In this case, the light beat is exploratory; it is then followed by a hard beat, which is the surprise action. Alternating the strength of the beat, or changing to the other side of the blade with a change-beat, helps to add variety to the preparation. Used prop-erly, it will lead the defender into wrongly guessing the final line of the attack, until it is too late.

4. Come on guard with the point out towards tierce (*see* Fig. 15). Bring the blade across towards the opponent's blade, without touch-ing. Then do a sudden beat attack very close to the blade. If the opponent launches an attack during the short pause, you have the option of a quick parry of quarte and riposte. The first action catches the opponent's attention. The attacker's blade gets precariously close to the defender's, paving the way for a sudden beat attack that is hard to stop.

Tierce is the third position and parry, protecting the upper right-hand side of the body. It was Le Perche de Coudray, in *L'Exercice des Armes ou le Maniement du Fleuret* (1635), who first assigned the name 'tierce' to this position.

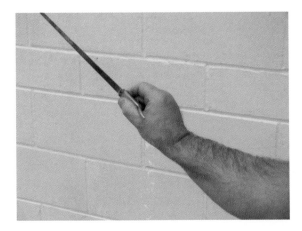

Fig. 15 Tierce (foil).

long (175mm), which places the beat inside the reaction time of the opponent: done properly this cannot be deceived. Beating the top of the blade is particularly useful at épée, as this exposes the upper forearm of the extended target. The épée beat uses a stronger turn of the hand, with the intention of knocking the opponent's point away from the attacker's knee. The efficiency of this advanced beat can be applied also to sabre, where beats can be delivered into the front, back and sides of the blade.

These are six classical ways I was taught to beat attack. I recall that at school, we were taught to ride a beat attack on the quarte side of the blade, rotating the blade through circular sixte, thus diverting the energy from the attacker's beat towards the defence.

The introduction of orthopaedic grips at foil brought about some changes. One of the more prominent actions, used to great effect, was the 'cutover beat'.

Cutover Beat
Orthopaedic foil grips these days are very common. However, when they first came out, many other fencers still used the French grip. It was quickly appreciated, however, that by using an orthopaedic grip fencers could obtain greater strength in their parries and attacks. Some masters concluded that it would harm classical fencing technique, since it could spoil good finger play. Early domination of the new grips in competitions made it easier for opponents using French grips to be disarmed; since then their popularity has grown. Its use at épée provides similar benefits, although some épéeists prefer a French grip, which can be held by the pommel to extend reach.

A particularly useful application of the orthopaedic versus French grip is the cutover beat.

5. Gather the blade with a circular sixte action. If the opponent evades the blade with a counter-disengagement, immediately roll the hand into a prime beat followed by cutover (molinello). If the molinello is evaded, the hand simply continues rotating to parry in sixte or tierce. This type of advanced action draws heavily on the classical Italian school of fencing, taking its inspiration from a circular action made from the sabre parry of prime.

A molinello, although normally associated with a cut made in sabre, can be used to effect in foil, based on the hand movements of a prime-tierce (or prime-high sixte) bind. The other way is to take the hand back a little, rotating it round on the prime side. It can be performed with or without contact with the opponent's blade and can be used as prise-de-fer, a beat, simple or compound attacks and as a riposte.

6. What follows is a highly advanced form of beat attack. The attacker stands on guard and lowers the point to the 5 o'clock position next to the opponent's guard, then rotates the hand to rapidly beat the blade on any of the four sides. The key to this whole operation is that the action must be no more than 7 inches

1. The attacker, using an orthopaedic grip, begins with a neat cutover, pauses momentarily (*see* Fig. 16), hovers and then beats downward on top of the blade (*see* Fig. 17) at an angle, moving his blade slightly forward. He applies

Fig. 16 The attacker pauses momentarily...

strong force, in such a way that the defender's weapon is taken out, between thumb and forefinger, and finishes with a lunge to target. The most important part of this action is the 'hover'. If you perform the cutover beat all in one go, you may be deceived. The hesitation is minute. Think of it like a runner at the starting blocks, waiting to explode into action.

Fig. 17 ...then beats downward, on top of the blade.

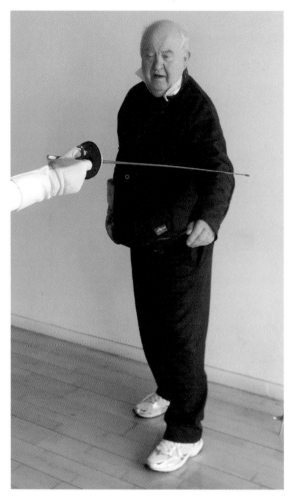

Fig. 18 The coach reaches forward with his left hand...

finger (*see* Fig. 19), causing the disarm (*see* Fig. 20). Traditionally, following the disarm, you would return your opponent's sword to him as it would be improper to take advantage of an unarmed man.

2. The attacker begins as before. This time, the opponent lunges into the preparation. In response, the original attacker beats the blade down to low left, with beat-parry and riposte, reacting defensively. The brief 'hover' provides an opportunity for the opponent to launch his attack. The original attacker's response is typically second intention.

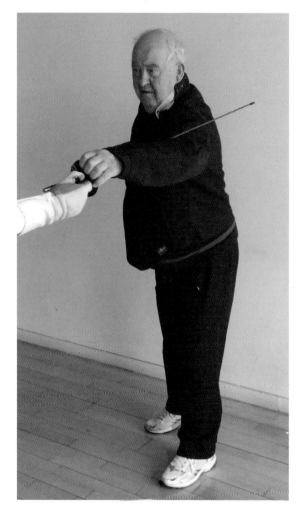

Fig. 19 ...applying a line of force between the thumb and forefinger...

The line of force is applied to the gap between thumb and forefinger, holding the French grip, causing the disarming of the foilist. This principle is similar to that used in a classical disarm, where the defender's armed, or unarmed, arm is wound around the attacker's blade, lifting it clear by breaking the grip between thumb and forefinger. The basic principles of a left-handed disarm are shown next. The coach reaches forward with his left hand (*see* Fig. 18), takes hold of the guard, applying a line of force between the pupil's thumb and fore-

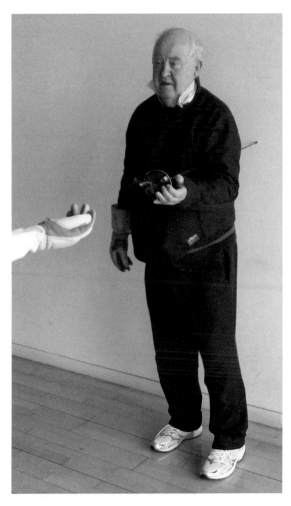

Fig. 20 ...causing the disarm.

fully, after presenting a straight arm aimed directly towards the target, clearing the poorly formed beat, this would be termed a dérobement. If the sword arm is bent, even though the beat is successfully deceived, the continuous attack which moves forward without hesitation should be awarded the hit. A successful outcome relies on the referee seeing things the same way. At advanced level, with a top-flight referee, this may be a justifiable risk.

4. The attack begins as before, this time beating under the blade with a movement of such force that the blade is driven upward, the point reaching head height as the attacker finishes with lunge to target. A defender, expecting a sudden beat downwards, may be caught unawares. This action is also good against an épéeist who fences with the point up. In a typical classical French épée lesson, the point is down. However, a fencer may have a reason for keeping the point raised. With the point in this position, the blade can be made to curve over the top of the guard to suddenly hit top wrist, which may demoralize an opponent.

Earlier, we looked at the simple parry of quarte – simple, only in the sense that the blade moves laterally, in the most direct path, to meet an attack or counter-attack. Now we will investigate circular parries.

Circular Parries

Circular parries, also known as counter-parries, describe a circular movement of the blade. Although generally this would be taken literally, F.C. Reynolds in *The Book of the Foil* has circular sixte illustrated with the point moving up and down in an elliptical shape, which is an alternative. The action and technique are very similar to a change of engagement in the same line, where the circular movement of the defender's blade returns to the original line of engagement to deflect the attacker's point from the target. Circular parries can be taken in the high-line, entirely using the fingers; or the low-line, where slight wrist action may be required. This basic technique is the same

3. The attacker begins as before. As he goes for the blade, the blade is deceived and the opponent begins to straighten his sword arm. The attacker continues with an attack to low-line. Both hits land. The attack is continuous, never stops moving forward, hence should be awarded the hit; but it could wrongly be given the other way. It may be possible to deceive the beat if it is poorly done, or anticipated. The attacker may have used this particular stroke too often, or without establishing the correct conditions. The opponent may have lifted his blade deliberately, to draw the attack, intending to deceive. If he does this success-

for foil and épée, although at épée the weapon is heavier and requires a firmer grip.

The word 'counter' is used in a number of contexts in fencing (counter-time, counter-disengagement, counter-offensive, counter-riposte), but the term 'circular' more accurately describes the nature of this parry.

The following exercises can also apply to simple parries:

1. In the classical circular parry of sixte the attacker's blade is transferred to the other side of the defender's blade by the tiniest of circular actions, manipulated by the fingers. To practise, the tip of the foil is placed on the inside of the defender's guard, the point projecting approximately 2 inches (50mm). The defender makes a small circular action transferring the attacker's blade to the outside, while resting in the on guard position, without the hand moving back. The riposte is direct. Careful practice is required in order to keep the size of the circle as tight as possible. This should be mastered to near perfection before proceeding to the other variations.

Generally, there are three feints around the foil and épée guards: at 1 o'clock, where the opponent is drawn to take a circular sixte parry; at 5 o'clock, which draws octave and may open up an opportunity for a low-high attack; and at 3 o'clock, with the point drifting horizontally, making circular sixte impossible and drawing quarte. An advanced fencer will know precisely where his point is at all times.

2. This time the attacker holds the point 6 inches (150mm) away from the defender's guard, then places it on the guard, as before. An alternative to this is to slide down the blade until the same position on the guard is reached. The defender carries out the small circular sixte parry with direct riposte. This preparatory movement creates a degree of uncertainty. The point held 6 inches away from the guard may drift to the right, removing the possibility of a circular parry, requir-

ing quarte; or it can drift below the guard, suggesting octave. A light sliding action down the blade might revert to a froissement, or detach suddenly.

The froissement is a grazing action on the opponent's blade, strongly and sharply bringing the forte of the attacker's blade diagonally from foible to middle, deflecting the opponent's blade sharply downward. More difficult to use than the beat, it requires a certain amount of force; if badly performed, it is easily deceived. Due to the characteristics of the froissement, it is best executed in quarte and tierce – unlike the pressure, or beat, which can be used in all fencing lines. A froissement is very useful from a low hand position, as this makes the defence of ceding parry more difficult.

3. The riposte may be angulated – typically in supination, with the thumb at 3 o'clock. Ripostes can be executed with opposition, or angulated opposition: good at close quarters, particularly against a flèche attack. Opposition ripostes are also much favoured by the épéeist.

Fencers may continue at close quarters when coming together, either accidentally or through design, and can still wield their weapons – without coming into contact as in corps à corps. Traditionally, this was discouraged as it made it difficult for a jury to follow. In the 1960s a combination of electric weapons and an aggressive fencing style increased its popularity and resulted in much body movement and highly angulated attacks. At close quarters, never step back. High-line parries are made with the hand lower; low-line parries with the hand higher. The blade is more vertical, reducing the chance of hitting off-target at foil. A step in parry is made a little wider, with the point already angulated towards the opponent's target.

It was also considered fair game to score a point by driving your opponent off the piste. Although well versed in classical technique, Bert was not averse to taking advantage of the modern interpretation of the rules. He once recounted a story about Charles de Beaumont who, at a foil competition, disapproved of him attempting to drive his opponent off the end of piste. Years later, Charles called fencers over to watch one of Bert's pupils, Lewis Smith, fence, saying words to the effect that this is how foil should be fenced.

4. After circular sixte the hand is lowered, with the thumb in the 1 o'clock position, or alternatively at 3 o'clock. The blade is positioned parallel to the floor, with the point facing close into the low-line. Here, the riposte is immediate. Supination is particularly useful against left-handers, where the hit can angulate onto the back.
5. After circular sixte the hand is lifted suddenly, riposting by dropping the point to an angle of about 45 degrees, which makes the riposte harder to parry. Dropping the point, taking it clear of the mask, is often used against a fencer who ducks.

All of the above apply equally to the circular parry of quarte.

Imagine a vertical line, descending from the sword arm side of the mask and intersecting with a horizontal line, extending from the armpit. This is the ideal spot that you are aiming for at foil. In the old days, masters had a little heart on their plastron in this position.

Circular parries of sixte and quarte can be changed by ending in the pronated positions of tierce and quinte. This opens up different parts of the target and allows for target selection.

6. If the circular parry of sixte reverts to tierce, the riposte can be to right shoulder, or with a flick to the low-line, or back – now harder since the changing of the foil timings. This is particularly useful when left- and right-handed fencers compete; the sudden use of tierce opens up the target. A lowered tierce is good for close quarters. From tierce, the riposte is delivered with a turn of the wrist.
7. The circular parry of sixte now reverts to raised sixte, by lifting the hand: a particularly good defence against a cutover or broken time attack. Some refer to this as the ninth blade position, or neuvième. The point descends and a neat riposte to back is possible, particularly if the attacker ducks down (*see* Fig. 21). Neuvième tended to be developed as a defence against a flick-hit to the shoulder. A variation against a left-handed opponent is,

Fig. 21 Circular sixte reverts to raised sixte, ripostes to back.

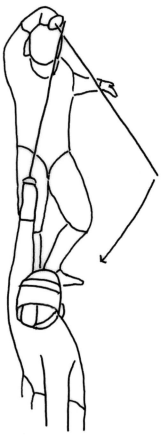

Fig. 22 Circular sixte rotates and lifts to prime, against a left-handed opponent.

after circular sixte, to keep rotating and lift to prime, which places the point precariously close to the left-hander's target. The riposte is completed by lifting the point, placing it neatly on target (*see* Fig. 22).

8. Standing on guard in sixte, release the blade to gravity; then pick it up fast, with the fingers, using circular sixte. This dramatic change of pace allows the defender to parry later, making the direct riposte faster on immediate contact with the blade. The change of speed in defence makes it more difficult for the attacker to deceive the blade, thus weeding out fencers with poor technique.

Like circular parries, the movement of the point with semicircular parries gives rise to their name. We will look at the semicircular parry of octave next.

Semicircular Parry of Octave

Semicircular parries, like octave, are usually taken from the high-line to the low-line, beginning in sixte and deflecting an attack to the low-line; but they can also be taken from the low-line to the high-line, beginning in octave and ending in sixte. Félix Gravé in *Fencing Comprehensive* refers to parries which are taken from high-line to low- or low-line to high-, on the same side, as corresponding parries.

The semicircular arc of the blade is achieved by rotating the wrist, assisted by the slight opening and closing of the last three fingers of the sword hand, which begins and ends with the thumb in the 1 o'clock position. The parry finishes on the same side of the body that it started. Also, octave can be used exceptionally to deflect an attack to the high-line at foil and épée. The use of octave in épée is quite specialized as it necessitates protecting the leg, which will be discussed later.

1. The classical approach to the semicircular parry of octave takes the form of a letter 'C', gathering the blade as the point goes for the low-line. If a low-high attack is executed, the option of successive parries to sixte, quarte or circular octave are available. A low-high attack, which drifts a little below then a little above the guard, is difficult to parry since the defender's blade movements are larger than those of the attacker, and the point is getting closer all the time.

2. An alternative to this is the 'U' shape on its side, allowing the fencer to parry an attack to the high-line with lots of opposition (*see* Figs 23–24), gathering the blade high and taking it low. The use of a semicircular parry of octave under these circumstances, as opposed to any typical high-line parry, is a surprise and not to be used habitually.

If an attacker takes your blade, the easiest defence is to take either a ceding or opposition parry, which follows.

Ceding and Opposition Parries

Ceding or yielding parries use the force of the

Fig. 23   A high line attack...

opponent's prise-de-fer to divert both the attacking and defending blades to another line, closing it defensively. No resistance is offered. Instead, you allow your foil to be taken from one line to another, forming the parry at the very last moment. The principal parries that can be made by ceding are quarte, prime and tierce. Prime can

sometimes be replaced with septime, quarte with quinte and tierce with sixte.

A prise-de-fer forces the opponent's blade from its existing line, carrying it into a new one. The three main examples are envelopment, bind and croisé. A prise-de-fer is only effective when the opponent's arm is extended, with the blade in

Fig. 24   ...is parried with octave.

line; it is most successful when the opponent has a rigid arm and strong wrist. Tactically, envelopment is most useful when the opponent's sword hand is relatively low; bind and croisé when it is high.

Compound prises-de-fer are two, or more, taken continuously without losing contact with the opponent's blade. Double prises-de-fer are two, or more, during which there is a momentary loss of the blade.

Apart from its use as a preparation for an attack, the bind can be effectively used to prepare a riposte against an attacker who, having been parried, tries to push through with a renewal of the attack. The bind dominates the blade, taking it into a different line. Binds can also be useful following low-line parries of octave and septime, where ripostes can sometimes be blocked by renewals of the attack. This is useful in épée, too.

Opposition parries progressively oppose the oncoming blade, directing the last part of a prise-de-fer away from the target. This technique requires accurate timing in lifting or lowering the point, in order to transfer the attacking foible into the defending forte. To be effective, the parry must be made as close as possible to the end of the attack.

In parrying, the important thing is to transfer domination of the blade from the opponent to you. This can only be done by bending your arm and raising or lowering your point, as required.

What follows are some other examples:

1. The attacker does slow circular sixte envelopment on the opponent's extended blade. When engaging the blade in sixte, rotate the wrist once, making the blade describe a circle as the arm is straightened. The version that I learned at school had two circular rotations; for a long time I referred to this as 'envelopment', but this would be more accurately described as 'double envelopment'. The ceding parry is typically taken to prime. High prime at foil is favoured by tall fencers, where the riposting point lands in the middle of the opponent's chest (*see* Fig. 25). The opposition parry is to tierce or sixte. Of the two, tierce is preferable as the use of sixte at foil, under these circum-

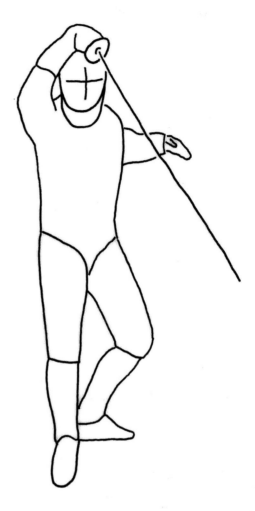

Fig. 25 High prime at foil is favoured by some tall fencers.

stances, can sometimes pick up an off-target hit on the arm. The clearance gained by using tierce is more pronounced and the sudden dropping of the point, with the riposte, most effective.

2. The attacker is on guard in octave and performs envelopment through circular octave on the opponent's extended blade. The ceding parry is to quarte or quinte. With

quinte, the riposte can be to the back. Quinte became popular with the introduction of electric scoring, as it took the point clear of the arm. It also helped that fencers in those days lunged with a high classical hand. The opposition parry is to tierce or sixte.

3. Beginning in quarte, the attacker takes the opponent's blade in septime and binds to sixte with a lunge. The ceding parry is to prime. The opposition parry is to tierce. Taking the blade in the middle of a fencing sequence is more effective than waiting for the opponent to helpfully extend his sword arm. The attacker must prepare the way.

4. An attack is made on the quarte side. The defender parries quarte and riposte with a coulé as the attacker returns to guard. Riposting with a coulé removes the possibility of the attacker's remise; this has become popular since the revision of the foil timings, where a sudden remise removes the riposting light. The ceding parry is to quarte. The opposition parry is to octave. Counter-riposte as required.

Poise and perfect balance are required to develop these skills. You can oppose in sixte and octave in foil, but tierce and seconde are much stronger.

The coulé is often underused in modern fencing, and may be described as a simple attack, attack on the blade, prise-de-fer, or even a feint. With its domination of the blade, it is useful at épée.

Having considered ceding and opposition parries with counter-ripostes, we will look at counter-ripostes in general, in particular the role of sixte.

Counter-ripostes

Counter-ripostes may be simple, compound or delayed. They can be delivered by either the attacker or defender. They are offensive actions, which follow the successful parry of a riposte or counter-riposte. Counter-ripostes can be taught in two ways – the coach can either parry the student's thrust, or let it first land then riposte.

A counter-riposte on the lunge tends to be simple, not compound, with quarte or sixte formed. It is done by moving the elbow towards the riposting blade and sword hand higher, in relation to the body, than when on guard. Immediate and simple, it has priority over any renewal of the original riposte. In a counter-riposte, which is second intention, the initial attack tends to be short, as we shall see.

Multiple counter-ripostes are numbered: the original attacker makes all the odd-numbered counter-ripostes and the original defender makes all the even-numbered counter-ripostes. This is a little academic, however, in this fast modern sport where multiple counter-ripostes are rare.

The first counter-riposte against a left-hander who takes quarte is often sixte, often a relatively weak parry. For many fencers, sixte is a panic reaction, so that an adequate counter-riposte does not materialize. Consequently, it must be practised assiduously, with close attention to detail.

A fencer with a strong parry of quarte and weak parry of sixte may expect an attack on the sixte side by an observant opponent, drawing the weak sixte parry. The alternative defence of circular quarte is slower. An efficacy in sixte is surely worth having. The exercises which follow, although following an inauspicious beginning, will take you there.

1. Start at straight arm distance to target (*see* Fig. 26). On the defender's opportunistic opening, the attacker simply extends his sword arm and hits. The defender parries sixte and ripostes direct (*see* Fig. 27). The original attacker parries sixte and counter-ripostes direct, without leaning forward, and hits on both arm extensions, which should be unhurried and smooth (*see* Fig. 28).

2. The first exercise is repeated, but as the original attacker parries sixte, with a view to counter-riposting direct, the original defender steps back (*see* Fig. 29), requiring a step to be added to the counter-riposte (*see* Figs 30–31). The fencers are still at straight arm distance to target. An alternative to offering an opening would be for the defender to apply pressure to the attacker's blade, creating a situation where the attacker starts with disengagement, extends his sword arm and hits.

Fig. 26 Start at
straight arm distance
to target.

Fig. 27 The attacker
extends and hits, the
defender parries sixte
and ripostes.

Fig. 28 The original
attacker parries sixte
and counter-ripostes.

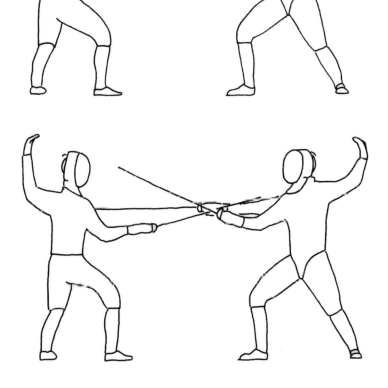

Fig. 29   The
original defender
steps back.

Fig. 30   A step
is added to the
counter-riposte...

Fig. 31   ...which
lands on target.

Fig. 32 The
defender steps back
with the opening.

Fig. 33 The
original attacker
steps back with
parry of sixte and
counter-ripostes.

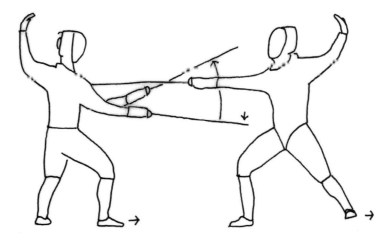

Fig. 34 The
attacker lunges for
the first time, with
the counter-riposte.

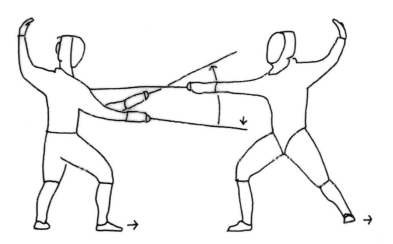

3. This time, the defender steps back with the opening (*see* Fig. 32), requiring the attacker to step forward with the initial extension of the sword arm and hit. The defender parries sixte and ripostes direct. The original attacker parries sixte and counter-ripostes direct. The fencer taking the counter-ripostes should be completely relaxed, concentrating on technique. The session is, as yet, very slow with the attacker hitting with both actions, but as confidence grows the opponent can occasionally parry the first hit.

4. The defender steps back with the opening, the attacker steps forward and extends; the defender parries sixte and ripostes with a step forward or lunge. The original attacker steps back with parry of sixte and counter-ripostes (*see* Fig. 33). The parry and counter-riposte is executed with the step back, ensuring that the hand is moving forward when the hit lands. If the counter-riposte is ill-timed with the step back, the hand will be moving back as the sword arm extends, thus losing aggression.

5. As before, the attacker steps forward on the first extension, as the defender keeps distance, parries sixte and ripostes – stepping back with the parry of sixte, stepping forward now with the counter-riposte. This is becoming progressively more difficult and requires additional powers of concentration. The emphasis should be on smoothness and correct technique, the body relaxed, upright at all times. They begin to move a little faster.

6. As before, but as the defender steps back, the attacker lunges for the first time with the counter-riposte (*see* Fig. 34). The lunge is made quickly, smoothly, without undue exertion. Gradually, these exercises develop aggressive, positive counter-riposting and a confidence in the use of sixte.

7. The attacker steps forward on the first extension. The fencers maintain distance, as the defender parries sixte riposte. The original attacker steps forward or backward, as required, parrying sixte and counter-riposting with a lunge. The attacker moves at an appropriate speed to read and respond to the defender's intentions, which varies the timing.

8. As before, but the original attacker finishes with sixte and counter-ripostes with a step and lunge. At the end of the lunge, the fencer's technique is correct: the point under complete control throughout and correct balance. The ability to respond to the opponent's actions developed slowly, always concluding with a neat hit.

9. When all of the above have been mastered, with different distances, the attacker may be allowed to finish with flèche (*see* Fig. 35) or balestra (*see* Fig. 36), incorporating a lunge.

Fig. 35 The attacker may be allowed to finish with a flèche...

Fig. 36 ...or
balestra.

What started as an undemanding extension of the sword arm has grown into an exercise where the use of distance, balance and poise must be maintained throughout.

A balestra is sometimes confused with a jump, or a hop. A hop is a short jump with both feet leaving the floor and landing at the same time, the weight evenly distributed between the feet. With the balestra, the initial kick of the front foot is like an appel, with the leg pulling the fencer's centre of gravity forward. But in the instant that the front foot slaps the floor, weight is removed from the rear foot, which is drawn forward, then replaced, in order to anchor the rear foot for the lunge. Done at speed, both feet land simultaneously; the space between them is the same as the guard position you started with, the distance covered being about the length of your foot. The body is now moving forward and the re kick of the front foot into the lunge is done with little effort, continuing this inertia – moving forward and down, never up and down, with no pause in the flow that might allow priority to be regained by the opponent attempting to place the point in line. One should only hear two sounds made by the feet: the first when landing forward, the second with the lunge. Some consider the balestra too perilous to use at épée, as it allows too much opportunity for counter-attack.

A balestra is also different from a bounce, which is a slight spring of the feet and arches, with minimum flexing of the knees. Like the hop, both feet leave the floor and land at the same time, with the centre of gravity equidistant between the feet, covering 6 to 8 inches (150 to 200mm). Bouncing forward moves you towards your opponent with greater speed than the classical advance and produces an element of surprise; it also hides your intentions from your opponent, as you may simply bounce on the spot, or bounce back, rather than launch an immediate attack. A bounce backward replaces the retreat, is as fast and as far as necessary to avoid being hit, or can launch an attack. With bouncing, the rear foot is not fixed as in classical footwork, which would restrict the fencer's ability to change direction. The fencer is never stationary, and is therefore harder to hit.

10. The attacker responds to pressure on the blade and, as the defender steps back, disengages and lunges to target (*see* Figs 37–39).
11. The defender varies distance, providing, when ready, an opening at straight arm distance to target, which he will meet with parry of sixte riposte. The attacker must be alert to this opening, then parry sixte, counter-riposting at the correct length. The original attacker gradually learns to choose between direct and indirect counter-ripostes and has developed an aggressive counter-riposte that puts pressure on the defender.

Fig. 37 The attacker responds to pressure on the blade, as the defender steps back...

Fig. 38 ... disengages...

Fig. 39 ...and lunges to target.

Fig. 40   The original attacker parries sixte on the lunge and counter-ripostes.

Fig. 41   After returning to guard, the original attacker parries sixte and counter-ripostes.

Fig. 42   The defender occasionally parries the first hit.

12. Now, the fencers begin at lunge distance to target. On the opening, the attacker lunges and hits. The defender parries sixte and ripostes. The original attacker parries sixte on the lunge and counter-ripostes (*see* Fig. 40).

13. Again, on the opening, the attacker lunges and hits; the defender parries sixte and ripostes, lunging when the attacker returns to guard. The original attacker parries sixte and counter-ripostes (*see* Fig. 41).

14. Now, the defender occasionally parries the first hit (*see* Fig. 42). When the original attacker returns to guard, he parries sixte (*see* Fig. 43) then counter-ripostes with a lunge as the original defender returns to guard (*see* Fig. 44). The original attacker is now making an aggressive, positive action. The counter-riposte from sixte, which started weak, is now familiar territory.

15. As before, but the original attacker's counter-riposte is delivered with step and lunge. The original defender maintains distance. If the body weight is wrong on the return to guard, there will be a delay in the step and lunge counter-riposte, with the original attacker vulnerable to redoublement.

16. At this point, the defender can vary the initial parry if he wishes, allowing the attacker the choice of parries and counter-ripostes.

17. After the initial lunge into the defender's opening, with his subsequent parry of sixte and riposte, the original attacker recovers forward, parries sixte (*see* Fig. 45), finishing the counter-riposte with a lunge. The hand position in sixte, with the arm extension, should now be well established from all the previous exercises.

18. Again, the original attacker's parry of sixte is made with a recovery forward; the counter-riposte is made with step and lunge. The attacker can now be allowed to make decisions about how to finish, depending on opponent's distance (step and lunge, balestra, flèche) or reactions (riposting direct or indirect).

19. Now, we can add second intention. The attacker should now have sufficient confi-dence to lunge at different speeds and draw a parry. The attacker lunges then three-quarter depth into the opening, allowing the defender to parry sixte and riposte, then parries sixte on the lunge and counter-ripostes crisply. The attack might follow a pressure on the sixte side of the blade, thus allowing the attacker to create the opening. A step forward and pressure, with the pressure coinciding with the landing of the rear foot, will help to drive the defender back, making a sixte riposte under pressure.

20. The attacker lunges three-quarter depth, following a pressure on the sixte side of the blade; the defender parries sixte and ripostes; the original attacker parries sixte on forward recovery and counter-ripostes. The depth of counter-riposte can be chosen according to conditions, always moving forward, perhaps forcing the defender to react against the blade, making an indirect counter-riposte possible.

We shall consider more indirect ripostes.

Indirect Ripostes

Indirect ripostes or counter-ripostes incorporate disengagement, cutover or counter-disengage-ment – the movement of the point about the blade being made before the extension of the sword arm. With disengagement, or cutover, the point passes into a new line. A counter-disengagement deceives a change of engagement, taken when returning to guard. All disengagements are a result of finger play. With the cutover, the sword arm is drawn back slightly, the forearm raised sufficient to clear the top of the opponent's blade and the sword arm quickly extended. With a riposte by cutover, the arm withdrawal is much greater owing to the closeness of the attacker, which may sometimes lead to a broken time riposte, landing in the same line as the parry when the attacker has taken his parry too fast. The cutover causes a break in the rhythm of the riposte.

At foil, great care must be taken to avoid the opponent's sword arm. At épée, this is not a constraint. Similar indirect ripostes can be

Fig. 43 The original attacker returns to guard...

Fig. 44 ...then counter-ripostes with a lunge.

Fig. 45 The original attacker recovers forward and parries sixte.

performed at sabre, but the hit can land with the point, as a cut, or even (in modern electric sabre) by a touching of the side of the blade.

1. We begin at lunge distance to body with the economic parry of quarte, described earlier. The attacker lunges; the defender parries quarte, at 1 o'clock. The attacker remains on the lunge, reacting to quarte, anticipating a direct riposte. The execution of the disengagement, as a riposte, is the same as with an attack, using the fingers: extending the sword arm, as the point descends, once you have entered into the new line. Early extension of the sword arm can lead to an off-target hit.

2. The next version starts off the same, but as the attacker returns to guard, the defender

completes the indirect riposte with a lunge. The lunge, which follows the extension of the sword arm, is a reaction to, not an anticipation of, the return to guard.

3. This time, the defender's parry of quarte is deliberately taken a little wide. The blade is then angulated, with indirect riposte to top shoulder; this is particularly good against a left-hander, where an indirect angulated riposte heads for the exposed target. As a fencer becomes more advanced, target selection has an increasing role to play.

4. Parry sixte against a left-hander, riposte immediately indirectly into the low-line, which goes below the left-hander's instinctive reaction parry of quarte. The low-line riposte can be delivered in pronation, the thumb at 9 o'clock, or supinated to 1 o'clock or 3 o'clock. Use a hand position you feel most comfortable with to guide your point.

5. Against a left-hander or right-hander, parry quinte, riposting immediately with cutover into the low-line. The point speed with the cutover is fast, leaving little reaction time for a parry. Using a lot of wrist, this is a very Italian type of indirect riposte. If the opponent moves in close, keep the arm bent; close proximity will make it even harder to parry.

6. This time the defender takes a very short parry of quarte; on making contact with the blade he immediately does an indirect riposte to the low-line; an opponent, attempting a reactive parry of quarte, will go straight over. It should be remembered that when this stroke was originally taught, if you met the blade the parry was given.

7. The defender parries high quarte, disengaging to shoulder, as the opponent reacts against the blade. The hand in high quarte is well placed for the indirect riposte to shoulder. The point drops onto the shoulder, avoiding the opponent's sword arm.

Fig. 46   On guard effaced.

8. The defender parries quarte; following the disengagement, he takes the opponent's blade, lunging with indirect opposition riposte as the opponent returns to guard. To practise this action effectively, the opponent raises the left hand and the defender aims his guard towards it when lunging with the indirect opposition riposte. This nicely removes the opportunity for the opponent to remise.

9. A classically trained fencer tends to come on guard effaced, as shown in Fig. 46 (the torso sideways, with the rear shoulder well back, showing less target), the realistic foil target reduced (*see* Figs 47–48). These are the target areas to which attacks are directed most frequently, because they are less easily defended. Here, a parry of quarte followed by a very pronounced angulated indirect riposte to the low-line can be very effective. The point is placed just under the elbow, making it difficult to parry.

The foil target for women used to stop at a line drawn between the top of the hips. This is shown in Eleanor and Ian MacDonald's *The Art of Fencing*. This situation changed in 1964, when it was made the same as the men's.

10. First, the defender begins on guard in quarte; the opponent lunges into the open line, staying on the lunge; the defender parries sixte and ripostes direct. Next, this is repeated but at the finish the attacker returns to guard, reacting against the defender's blade. The defender neatly does disengagement, riposting indirectly, with a lunge.

11. This time, as the attacker returns to guard, reacting against the defender's blade, the defender turns the sword hand in pronation, thumb at 9 o'clock, riposting indirectly into the low-line.

12. As before, but as the attacker returns to guard, he attempts a circular change of engagement to quarte; the defender responds with a counter-disengagement indirect riposte, with lunge. To practise, the attacker stays on the lunge, slowly returning to guard with the change of engagement, while the defender

Fig. 47 The realistic foil target – front.

does the counter-disengagement, ensuring that the sword arm is straight, before the lunge begins.

13. Once more, the opponent lunges into the open line. The defender parries sixte, but this time bears down on the blade, in supination, thumb at 3 o'clock. This time, as the

Fig. 48 The realistic foil target – back.

attacker reacts against the defender's blade, the defender neatly does a cutover, riposting indirectly to the low-line. This is sometimes called a flying cutover, which is a combination of a beat and backward glide along the opposing blade, followed by the cutover. It is particularly effective if the defender closes distance, hitting at close quarters; done suddenly, it is difficult to parry.

14. The defender parries circular sixte and ripostes indirectly into the low-line, in pronation, thumb at 9 o'clock.

15. The defender parries circular sixte and ripostes indirectly into the low-line, in supination, thumb at 3 o'clock.

16. The defender comes on guard, with the blade parallel to the floor, which is sometimes referred to as the Polish Parallel Guard. The attacker lunges to target. The defender lifts the sword hand with a sharp circular sixte parry, rotating immediately on contact, in the opposite direction, with an indirect riposte – all in one continuous movement.

17. The defender parries raised sixte and ripostes indirectly to the trunk of the opponent's body, with the hand still in the supinated parry position. This provides tremendous angulation to the riposting blade, making it difficult to parry. If the attacker drops his wrist after the defender's parry, the riposte is even easier.

18. Now, parry raised sixte and riposte indirectly to left shoulder, again adding to the problem of making a successful parry with target selection.

19. Parry raised sixte, preparing the way for a

supinated riposte. The attacker takes back his hand, anticipating the parry, breaking his timing. The opportunity now exists for the defender to perform an evasive manoeuvre of inquartata, often accompanied with a stop-thrust – a potential championship-winning stroke.

Inquartata, incorporating a stop-thrust, a counter-attack in the same line as the attacking blade, is from the Italian school. The left leg is extended backward (as in a reverse lunge) and left foot shifted approximately 45 degrees to the right of the line of direction. The rear arm stays behind and in line with the sword arm to maintain balance. The toe of the right foot remains pointing forward. The body target is thus displaced away from the attacker's point. It is essential that you do not displace the head, rise during this sudden slanting movement or give the slightest indication of your intention. The counter-offensive action may be by detachment, opposition to the blade, angulated or renewed. Aldo Nadi in *On Fencing* describes the position of the legs at the conclusion as being bent more than in the normal guard position, as opposed to the version described above (*see* Figs. 49–52). William Gaugler in *The Science of Fencing* describes the use of inquartata at sabre against the attacker's point thrust to inside chest, or cut to head or left cheek; the counter-offensive action is applied with point to the attacker's chest, or cut to left cheek.

We have studied the role of prise-de-fer and the defence of ceding and opposition parries. Now, we will examine the role of a particular type of prise-de-fer: the croisé.

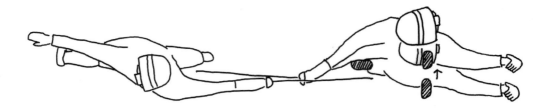

Fig. 49   The rear foot moves back, in the on guard position.

Fig. 50 The body target is displaced away from the attacker's point.

Croisé

A taking of the blade which transports the opponent's blade from high- to low-line, or low- to high-line, taken on the same side as the engagement, is by its nature a defensive action. Whilst low- to high-line is theoretically possible, lack of control of the opponent's point makes it too dangerous. The sixte croisé is seldom used, except against left-handers. This leaves us typically with the quarte croisé.

Fig. 51 This can be done with opposition...

Fig. 52   ...and may incorporate a reverse lunge.

Think of the croisé as an entrapment of the blade. Years ago there was a notch in the guard of a foil specifically for this purpose. The defence against a croisé is an opposition parry.

1. The classical approach to the crois starts as the attacker lunges to high-line. The defender parries quarte; pivots the blade over the attacker's, by turning the hand, still in half-supination, at 1 o'clock; then bears down on the blade, lowering the wrist and forearm (*see* Figs 53–55). Lastly, the blade is angulated towards the low-line – all this, ideally taken when the attacker's blade is still moving forward. This approach takes the point clear of the original attacker's leg.

2. The modern approach to the croisé starts as before. The defender parries quarte; pivots the blade over the attacker's by turning the hand in half-supination; then turns the hand in pronation, by moving through quinte, finishing in the low-line. The modern version is a little faster, but risks a percentage of hits landing on the leg. It is also possible to draw the point onto your own leg. It lends itself to a very effective time-thrust through quinte.

As with all time-thrusts, the success depends on correctly anticipating which line the attack will end.

3. A classical sixte croisé can be used against a left-hander. The attacker lunges to the high-line, the defender parries sixte, pivots the blade over the attacker's by turning the hand, still in half-supination; then bears down on the blade, lowering the wrist and forearm. Lastly, the blade is angulated towards the low-line. Straightening the arm, while dropping the hand, would turn this action into a time-thrust.

The popularity of the remise, with the current timings of the electric box, demonstrates the validity of the croisé in the modern game.

Earlier, we considered a situation where the defender came on guard with the blade parallel to the floor. We will explore this further.

Polish Parallel Guard

The foil on guard position that I was taught was typically with the point at mouth or eye level. Bac H. Tau, in *Fencing Volume Two, The Foil* has the point at shoulder level. However, he offers

Fig. 53 The defender parries quarte...

two variations: the Offensive On Guard Position, where the point is lowered to hand level, with the blade parallel to the floor, when fencing further apart; and the Defensive On Guard Position, where the point is raised to eye level, or higher (more useful at close quarters). An on guard position where the blade is held parallel to the ground is sometimes referred to as the Polish Parallel Guard. Holding the blade parallel to the floor removes the opportunity for the attacker to make beat attacks on the sides of the blade; also, the blade is already pointed towards the general target area.

The following exercises will help you understand what is possible from this position:

1. Start at straight arm distance to target. The attacker stands on guard, with the blade

parallel to the floor. The defender goes for the blade, laterally, on either side. The attacker does disengagement, straightening the sword arm and hitting the target; as the point is already lowered, this action is quicker than usual.

2. The same exercise is then carried out at lunge distance to target. Once again, this action is quicker than usual. The sword arm straightens immediately into the lunge, without hesitation.

3. From this on guard position, it is possible to launch a very sudden high or low level attack, as the point moves forward quickly. A low-line attack is more dangerous because the attack is now much shorter, particularly if the point is just below the guard, the blade movement of the low-line parry larger by comparison. If

Fig. 54 ...pivots the blade over the attacker's...

Fig. 55   ...then bears down on the blade.

the defender responds with a high-line parry, the attacker finishes in the low-line. If the defender responds with a low-line parry, the attacker finishes in the high-line.

4. Beats on top or below the blade come into their own from this position. The beat is short and sudden. A flèche can be introduced, if the defender attempts to retreat just outside lunge distance. If the defender takes a late parry a tiny disengagement, or counter-disengagement, close to the target can lead to a hit.

5. Some types of defences can be very fast and very late. With the blade parallel to the floor, the parry of circular sixte is smaller, which allows it to be taken faster and much later.

6. Similarly, the parry of octave is also smaller, since the point is already lowered, which allows the parry to be taken much later. Whilst quarte may be taken from this position, there is little advantage to be gained since the point must first be lifted.

7. Because the blade is already horizontal, lifting it to raised sixte comes naturally.

8. The defender can delay parries because they are shorter, adding to the threat of a swift riposte when the attacker's target is precariously close. The lateness of parries means that successive parries are less likely to be needed, but if required may be taken from this position: sixte-quarte, octave-quarte, octave-counter octave, etc.

Because of the sudden, effective control applied to the blade, this approach is purpose-made for the orthopaedic grip. Another position that lends itself to the orthopaedic grip is the Italian guard, which follows.

Italian Guard

In the French guard, the sword arm is half extended, with the elbow clear of the body, as in sixte. In the Italian guard, the hand is further forward, turned in pronation, with the point extended a little to the right, as in tierce.

Including the pommel, the French handle is about 8 inches long (200mm) and slightly curved to fit the palm of the hand. The traditional Italian handle is shorter, and straight, with a cross-bar just behind the guard. This cross-bar offers a more secure grip of the weapon. The orthopaedic foil grip lends itself more to this style of fencing than the French grip.

The French guard is susceptible to a direct coulé – also a disengagement thrust, which starts the same. This is one of the principle weaknesses of the French on guard position. The Italian guard removes the option of the coulé, because the point is slightly to one side. Here, point speed is faster than the traditional French school attack. The Italian school is about taking and dominating the blade; the French school, more about the art of deception.

Fig. 56   On guard in tierce.

Fig. 57   Riposte from tierce.

Begin as follows:

1. Start at straight arm distance to target. Both fencers stand on guard in tierce. One fencer touches the outside of the other's blade by extending the sword arm and rotating the wrist. On contact, the other turns the sword hand from the pronated position, dominating the blade and suddenly dropping the point onto the target (*see* Figs 56–57). If you are not used to it, this can be a difficult exercise and should be developed progressively.

2. Next, the same exercise is performed at lunge distance. One fencer does a short lunge, touching the outside of the other's blade, then returns to guard. On contact, the other responds as before, straightening the sword arm, lunging in response to the other's return to guard. The emphasis, as before, is on strong domination and opposition with the blade. The hit is stressed with this action, consequently the point stays on a little longer, which is very relevant to modern box timings: never 'punch' the hit at your opponent, but press with the thumb to place the point accurately.

3. This action can be used with a flèche, if the opponent attempts to retreat out of foil lunge distance. The emphasis here is on a terrific turning of the wrist. This direct action suddenly becomes dangerous.

4. With a circular tierce parry and riposte direct, the point speed becomes phenomenal. The attacker lunges to the inside of the guard, allowing the circular parry to be taken, staying on the lunge. The defender's whole action

is taken continuously, with total domination of the blade. The strong circular wrist action is finished with the thumb, to ensure the point bites. When being instructed in this, the only response I could come up with was a ceding parry of prime, which was too late.

Against a flèche attack, a tierce riposte has a lot of force as the blade turns in.

With the French guard, against a very high attack, a quarte riposte was not always given. In the early days of electric boxes, 'presidents', as referees were then called, reacted to the sequence of lights. The expression 'continuation of the attack' came into fashion, rather than talking about the 'remise', which is the correct classical interpretation. Fencers and coaches began to realize that the Italian pronated foil parries of tierce and quinte had value.

With the parry of quinte, the point is a little raised, nearly parallel to the ground. The riposte is delivered with thumb and finger, with opposition, in the low-line. Properly executed, this sudden domination can take a French grip out of an opponent's hand, and often did during Bert's demonstrations.

Disengagement to a defender's quarte can lead to circular quarte, ending in quinte – effectively stopping a one-two attack.

In the French guard, parrying seconde (from sixte) can lead to the elbow sticking out. To avoid this, move the hand slightly forward and the elbow will stay in. When parrying seconde (from tierce) with the Italian guard, the elbow is more likely to stay in.

1. The defender stands on guard in tierce. The attacker lunges to low-line, causing the defender to parry seconde; he ripostes direct, with opposition on the blade, the use of the thumb and forefinger preceding the hit. With this sharp wrist action and the hand slightly forward, it is possible to make a very fast riposte.
2. As before, but the defender does riposte with disengagement, over the top of the blade – the target is wide open.
3. Next, the defender does riposte with a low-line cutover: the blade coming in sideways to the attacker's target, at an angle that is difficult to parry. This sudden flick over the blade, using the wrist, is excellent at close quarters.
4. When the blade is presented in line, or half in line (arm semi-extended), a very fast preparation – by engagement of seconde followed by an attack by disengagement – is very strong. When this was demonstrated to me, my French foil grip flew away from my hand.
5. For an attack of low-high, a good French school defence may be successive parries of octave and then taking a diagonal parry to quarte, also referred to as cutting-the-line. But in the Italian guard, the response is a very decisive seconde-tierce, with strong movement of the wrist: easy and effective.
6. The defender comes on guard in seconde and the attacker lunges into the high-line. The defender takes circular seconde, riposting with full opposition on the blade. This is an elliptical gathering action in the character of prise-de-fer, taking hold of the blade and momentarily weakening the attacker's grip: very effective against a flèche attack.
7. The defender parries seconde and ripostes with a coulé, as the attacker returns to guard. This riposte can be direct or, if the original attacker reacts by lowering his sword arm, the finish can be disengagement into the high-line.
8. The defender parries seconde against a lunge into the low-line and ripostes with envelopment. When the blade is still taken, the sword arm is still bent, until domination is achieved; then the arm is extended with strong opposition on the blade. If the original attacker resists, disengagement may be incorporated at the end. In the French school, the defender's parry can be taken in octave (rather than seconde), with strong lift and angulation: excellent when close. If the opponent ducks down, the lift can revert to the back.

9. At lunge distance, against the opponent's straight-arm presentation of the blade, the attacker beats in seconde and attacks over the top to the high-line. The hand turns into the beat and spins back, the wrist brought into play on both actions, imparting terrific point speed to the attack.

10. The attacker, on guard in seconde at lunge distance, lifts the point to feint to target. The defender is in sixte. On the defender's blade reaction, the attacker does a cutover lunge. There is no break in timing, because of the speed of the wrist. The initial threat is on the sixte side, leaving the quarte side vulnerable.

11. Next, the attacker, on guard in seconde, feints quickly, just under the blade. When the defender takes circular sixte, he follows the blade around and finishes in the low-line. This is called a doublé – a feint of disengagement – which draws the circular parry and is then deceived by a counter-disengagement. The attacker's hand is already in the correct position; the point moves quickly around the guard, finishing in the low-line.

12. The attacker, on guard in seconde, lunges to the low-line. The defender, on guard in sixte, parries octave successfully. The attacker immediately renews the attack, with redoublement to the high-line, with a sudden twist of the wrist.

13. The same sequence can be performed, but after the defender parries octave successfully, attempting a riposte into the high-line, the redoublement is now applied with opposition against the riposting blade.

With electric scoring, the parry of octave tends to leave the attacker's point in line with the leg as the riposte arrives. Traditional scoring, with judges, would tend to favour the riposte. A white off-target light adds ambiguity to the phrasing – in some cases, preventing the riposte from being given. The problem can be resolved by using seconde, which lifts the attacker's point away from the leg.

The continuity hitting exercises which follow are evocative of the Italian school:

14. The defender parries tierce; riposte direct to chest; riposte indirect with a disengagement to chest, indirect with a cutover to chest, and finally indirect with a counter-disengagement to chest.

15. The defender parries quinte; riposte direct to flank; riposte indirect with disengagement to chest, indirect with a cutover to flank, and finally indirect with a counter-disengagement to chest.

16. As before, but the defender parries and ripostes standing still on the first action; lunges with the riposte and recovers on the second action; parries and ripostes standing still, on the third action; and lunges with the riposte and recovers on the fourth action.

Bert originally took lessons with an Italian foil with a cross-bar. The orthopaedic grip lends itself to this style better than the French grip ever did. In the mid-1970s, the Dingwall Academy school club (north of Inverness) still fenced with Italian foils. This school under the guidance of teacher John Fleck went on to produce British champions.

We have considered redoublements in connection with the Italian guard; now we will examine them in relation to the French on guard position of sixte.

Redoublements

A redoublement is an immediate renewal of the attack, without rising from the lunge, or by lunging or flèche after returning to guard. It is made into the same or a different line to which the blade was parried. This is achieved by additional movements of the blade, arm or body and is useful against a fencer who hesitates on a parry.

Be careful not to use renewal of attacks routinely. A beginner may exploit renewals due to a weakness in defence and learn bad habits.

In the early days of electric foil, the blades were unwieldy; it was no easy task to place a riposte successfully. Consequently, the attacker would often jab at the lower target until a hit arrived. During this period, the odds favoured the redoublement. Now, since the changing of the box timings to eradicate the flick-hit, the odds once again favour the redoublement.

1. The attacker lunges short and then does a redoublement, with disengagement, as the defender moves forward.
2. The defender is on guard in sixte; the attacker lunges to the low-line; the defender parries octave successfully, with a pause. The original attacker immediately does a redoublement to high-line, with opposition on the blade as the defender moves forward. This is effectively a time-thrust through sixte. Leaning in a little with the redoublement provides more depth and increases the opposition. Leaning in tends to eliminate the possibility of a compound riposte: not pretty, but effective.
3. Against a left-handed fencer, lunge low; the defender parries octave. As the defender lifts the blade and moves forward, time-thrust through quinte, taking the hit into the left-hander's open line.
4. As before, but against a right-handed fencer, time-thrust through quinte; the hit ends up in the right-hander's low-line.

All of the above are second intention.

Like redoublements, remises are another form of second intention: renewed offensive actions.

Remises

In the classical sense, a remise is a renewal of the attack, in which the blade remains in the line in which it was parried or missed; it is then replaced on target, or left in line for an opponent to advance onto. It is useful against an opponent who makes a riposte which is delayed, indirect or compound, à temps perdu (with loss of fencing time). However, over the years a renewal of attack involving a slight movement of the shoulder, combined with angulation of the blade, has been introduced. A purist would call this a redoublement, but we will call all of the following examples remises.

In *The Complete Guide to Fencing* by Barth/

Beck (Ed.), remise attacks (as they are referred to) are divided into 'direct', 'disengagement' and 'sweep'. Direct remise attacks may be executed with a straight thrust or angulated thrust, as in the case of the previous example. Disengagement remise attacks are usually performed from further away, which makes the renewal into the uncovered opening possible: additional footwork, extended lunge – dragging the back foot forward in the lunge and flèche out of the lunge – may be necessary. In sweep remise attacks, the opponent dodges an attack by moving back and presenting the line. A direct remise is not possible, as priority has passed to the opponent; hence the blade needs to be deflected. Unlike direct remises, where the point is basically left out for the opponent to move onto, the others involve movement of the blade or foot; a purist, in the French classical tradition, would call these redoublements.

Ramon Castellote in *The Handbook of Fencing* suggests that a remise is made when the opponent releases your blade too early, to make a feint of riposte, prior to you returning to guard. The remise is administered without recovering from the lunge, but by making a slight backward inclination of the body to suggest to the opponent that you are returning to guard. As this involves a slight blade movement, a purist might also think of this as a redoublement.

Remises and redoublements tend to be actions, at foil, which are more effective on the quarte/septime side, where the sword arm is not likely to get in the way. An épéeist, having made an unsuccessful attack to wrist, may remise to upper arm or body.

1. The attacker does disengagement, lunges to target, and is parried. Staying on the lunge, the point is left out – relying on the defender's feet moving forward prematurely, responding compound, or broken time, for the point to land. Early observations of your opponent's reactions will lead you to select such a stroke. Those wishing to avoid the indignity of being hit by a remise may well wish to consider the advice of George Roland in *A Treatise on the Theory and Practice of the Art of Fencing*, who

wrote: 'If the eye and wrist precede the foot, the execution will be just.'

2. The attacker does disengagement with a lunge and is parried in quarte. On the defender's hesitation, the attacker remises, by moving the shoulder a little forward and angling suddenly around the parry of quarte. This can be achieved with or without moving the front foot forward. The defender is left with few options – one being to attempt a time-hit through quinte.

3. This time the attack is on the sixte side of the blade, with a lunge, which is parried. On the defender's hesitation, the attacker remises, by moving the shoulder a little forward and angling suddenly around the parry of sixte, with or without moving the front foot forward. This and the previous exercise may be initiated by starting deliberately with a short lunge, then remising by moving the front foot forward, effectively making this second intention.

4. The attacker does disengagement with a lunge and is parried in octave. The defender begins a slow riposte to the high-line. The attacker remises to the low-line in pronation, dipping the body down: useful against a taller opponent.

5. The attacker does disengagement with a lunge and is parried in quarte. The taller defender attempts to riposte to the back. The attacker remises to the low-line, in pronation, ducking down.

6. The attacker lunges and is parried in tierce. The defender's riposte is suddenly down the blade, using thumb and forefinger. The original attacker's only response available is the ceding parry of prime. The original defender immediately remises with angulation, around the parry. With the point facing the floor, in prime, it is difficult to make any kind of quick reaction. When riposting from tierce, an orthopaedic grip is advantageous for sliding down the blade effortlessly.

Remises, like redoublements, can be practised followed by parries, so that only one hit lands. Used classically against a compound riposte,

they are also effective against a simple riposte, provided these are avoided or parried.

Next, we will look at counter-time.

Counter-Time

Roger Crosnier in *Fencing with the Electric Foil* makes a subtle distinction between defensive and offensive counter-time. With defensive counter-time the fencer draws a stop-hit, parries and ripostes; the intention is to prepare the way for the riposte. With offensive counter-time the fencer's intentions are, from the start, more aggressive, looking all the time for an opportunity to launch an attack. Counter-time provokes an offensive or counter-offensive reaction, so that it can be opposed with a riposte or an attack.

These principles apply also to épée and sabre, but the target selection will vary, as will the nature of the hit at sabre.

1. The attacker takes a (deliberately) small step forward, is attacked on the preparation, parries quarte and ripostes. This is defensive counter-time.

2. The attacker beats the blade, immediately straightening the sword arm; then momentarily withdraws his sword hand, drawing an attack on the preparation, parries quarte and ripostes. This is defensive counter-time.

3. The attacker begins an attack, with the sword arm bent, drawing a stop-hit. The attacker does a beat-attack on the quarte side of the blade, in mid-lunge. This is offensive counter-time.

A foil parry that became fashionable, and remains so, follows next: prime.

Prime

Originally a parry or position assumed when a sword is drawn from its scabbard – perhaps in response to an attack – that protects the left-hand side, prime is useful in close-quarters fighting (*see* Fig. 58). Protecting mainly the fencer's inside high-line, it is seldom used as the basis of an attack in modern fencing. There are many variations in the height of prime.

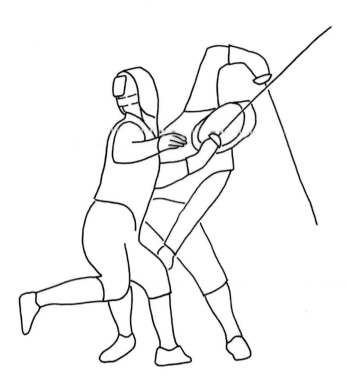

Fig. 58 Prime at close quarters.

1. The attacker begins with a slow straight thrust to the high-line; the defender parries prime and ripostes directly by lifting the point towards the target. The parry is taken sufficiently high, so that the defender has a clear view under the sword hand, where the riposte lands.

2. The attacker slides down the sixte side of the blade. The defender cedes to prime and ripostes, as before.

3. The attacker does disengagement and then counter-disengagement as the defender parries circular sixte. The defender reverts to prime and ripostes directly. If the blade is found in circular sixte, the action continues as prise-de-fer.

4. A right-hander fencing a left-hander: the right-handed defender's shoulder appears exposed. The left-handed attacker directs his point to this apparently undefended area, the defender lifts his sword hand to prime with a minimal movement and ripostes directly. Alternatively, the defender lifts the sword hand to prime and attempts a time-thrust, more or less in one action.

5. If an attacker ducks down to cover target, after a defender's successful parry of prime, this provides a good opportunity for a riposte on the back – particularly useful to a taller defender. With 'steam foil' this would never have been seen, but with electric foil the hit is registered.

6. The defender begins in octave with the attacker's high level attack, parries prime and ripostes directly. The same action can be performed from seconde. Next, come on guard in quarte and perform the same parry and riposte. Begin in raised sixte with the attack, gather in prime and riposte directly. The height of the attack determines the height of the prime parry. Practise prime from every position in order to gradually build up confidence.

7. Attack to the upper target, which is parried by the opponent; return to guard and counter-riposte from prime.

8. Next, the attacker lunges a little short (deliberately, with second intention); when the opponent responds with a flèche, the original attacker returns to guard, parries prime and

Fig. 59   In épée, the riposte…

riposte directly. **Prime is better than quarte** under these circumstances; the distance between the fencers is closing rapidly, but the target is still wide open.

Prime, a pronated parry like seconde and tierce, may be used at foil and épée. It is particularly effective against someone trying to force their way with angulation around the defender's blade. In épée the riposte is more likely to end up on the leg (*see* Figs. 59–60). Its classical use in sabre as part of the First Defensive Triangle (prime-seconde-quinte) is well known, but much has changed in sabre.

Fig. 60   …is more likely to end up on the leg.

2 Sabre

Introduction

Electronic scoring in sabre was not developed until the late 1980s; previously, hits had been judged visually. 'Steam' sabre, as it would later be referred to, had an off-target area from the waist down, which, if hit, would stop the fight – not unlike foil. This was discarded in favour of a much simpler system, where the fencers wore lame jackets, connected to masks, and where a simple touch scored a hit, with no distracting off-target. The hit, which at 'steam' sabre was characterized by an actual sabre cut or point, no longer applied. Instead, touching the blade in such a way as to make electrical contact allowed the referee to award the hit. Another important change was the abolition of the flèche, or cross-step forward, which was done to remove the tendency for simultaneous attacks. A more detailed explanation of the impact of electronic scoring is available in Zbigniew Borysiuk's *Modern Saber Fencing*.

On the traditional side, Zoltán Beke's and József Polgár's *The Methodology of Sabre Fencing* is exceptional – a book for coaches, extolling the

Fig. 61 'A' Grade at Crystal Palace, London 2011, Women's Team Sabre. Min Zhu (China), left, and Ibtihag Muhommed (USA). (Photo: Graham Morrison)

virtues of the classical Hungarian sabre fencing system, one of its most significant features being their regular notes on 'Most Frequently Occurring Points' and 'Corrective Exercises'. Also, a slimmer volume, D.F. (Derek) Evered's *Sabre Fencing*, is worth a mention; it also predates electric sabre fencing. I corresponded with Derek in 2004 regarding his review of *Fencing: Essential Skills Training* written for the newsletter of Egham Fencing Club, *Cut and Thrust*. His book, although heavily criticized at the time of publication, is still worthy.

Notwithstanding the many changes in the character and execution of modern sabre fencing – for example, the increasing percentage of hits landing on the upper arm and forearm – the traditional approach to training still gives the broadest of preparations.

We shall start with the simple act of how to grasp the sabre.

The Grip

1. The classical sabre grip is well documented. It is held with the fingers against the heel of the hand: the ball of the thumb on top of the handle, as flat as possible, about ½ inch (12mm) clear of the guard; the tip of the thumb level with the second phalanx of the index finger. The other fingers bend freely around the handle, holding it flexibly. The grip is correct when the hand does not clench the handle; the sabre should be held in a relaxed manner, alternating between looser and firmer grips, and the palm empty (*see* Fig. 62).

2. In another variation, which was taught by Alf Simmonds, the grip is thrown forward, with the thumb extended a little further forward (*see* Fig. 63). The resulting cut accelerates, due to the exaggerated thumb action. When first encountering electric sabre fencing, Bert found this extremely effective. Also, this grip tends to avoid heavy hitting, because you are lifting the elbow rather than throwing from the shoulder.

The speed of sabre bouts require a delicate, yet flexible, hold on the weapon. Parries, beats and

Fig. 62   The classical sabre grip.

Fig. 63   Alf Simmonds' grip.

stop-hits require a firmer grip, whereas attacks with feints and counter-attacks require a looser grip. You may have to squeeze a little with your thumb and index finger to keep the sabre from dropping out of your hand, but you should keep the grip as loose as you can.

The correct manipulation of the weapon is referred to in Léon Bertrand's *The Fencer's Companion*, where he refers to 'sabre in hand' – *sciabola in mano* – by which he means controlled and conserved strength, the elimination of force and the ability to check the edge of the sabre on impact. He considers the practice of the circular cut, known as the 'molinello', an invaluable adjunct in developing these skills. The molinello has previously been referred to in connection with foil, but originates in Italian sabre. In this circular cut the blade, forearm and point describe a complete or part circle. Molinelli may be horizontal, diagonal or vertical.

The introduction of the electric sabre has created a vulnerable area between elbow and shoulder. The most natural response to this is to move the hand over a little to compensate.

Now, how to stand on guard.

On Guard

Classically trained fencers would take fencing lessons from different guards and not mix them up. This later reverted to two on guard positions: tierce, a defensive position, and secondly the offensive–defensive position of tierce, with the blade rotated in alignment with the left shoulder. From tierce, the attack to head is telegraphed, since it cannot be executed without first turning the hand. In the offensive–defensive position, the hand is held well forward, allowing the attacker to launch an attack without warning, yet being able to fall back on tierce if attacked. This is best illustrated in Roger Crosnier's *Fencing with the Sabre*. The manipulation of the sabre is shared by the fingers and the wrist, never the wrist on its own. Today, a modern on guard position is likely to have the blade presented facing forward, or even with the guard turned completely round in tierce, protecting the forearm. The need to present a cutting edge to score a hit no longer applies. When electric sabre was first introduced, left-handers would be fenced in tierce, since with the new form of scoring the shoulder was exposed to hits from left-handers. This helped to cut out the whip.

A classic tierce on guard position has certain characteristics. The guard and blade are turned, protecting the knuckles, forearm, upper arm and cheek. The trunk of the body is erect, with the feet at right angles. Some modern fencers have modified this basic position: the feet do not form a 90-degree angle and they prefer the rear foot to point slightly forward, with the trunk and hips slightly inclined forward, loading the front leg.

László Szabó, in *Fencing and the Master*, describes the requirement for all positions to be a natural body and trunk bearing, with loose muscles – a readiness to move, with constant stability. He describes the arms as virtually dangling from the shoulders. These positions may be adapted to permissible deviations from the proper positions of the pelvis and feet, due to individual differences in physical build, fencing position and lunge.

Stop-cuts are considered next, which are counter-offensive actions made into your opponent's attack or counter-attack.

Stop-Cuts

Most stop-cuts in the UK are likely to be taken from tierce. However, classically trained fencers were taught to stop-cut from every position. The example which follows shows an angulated stop-cut from quarte (*see* Figs 64–65). The parry was always correctly formed, the speed of the stop-cut achieved by using the fingers. Great use of the feet was necessary to maintain a period of fencing time to separate the stop-cut from the attack. By careful application of the fingers, it was possible to stop-cut twice in time. It should be remembered that a stop-cut is a planned action of second intention, not done as a reaction; it is possible to remise a stop-cut.

1. Begin at step and lunge distance to head and body. The defender stands on guard. The attacker steps forward, presenting for a lunge to flank; the defender moves to tierce. Instead of maintaining the parry, the fencer counter-attacks. He stop-cuts with angulation to the top of the attacker's wrist, stepping backward, clear of the attacker's blade.
2. As before, but this time the attacker steps forward, presenting for a lunge to chest; the defender moves to quarte. Instead of maintaining the parry, the fencer counter-attacks. He stop-cuts with angulation to inside of the attacker's wrist, stepping backward, clear of the attacker's blade.
3. As before, but this time the attacker steps forward, presenting for a lunge to head; the defender moves to quinte. Instead of maintaining the parry, the fencer counter-attacks. He stop-cuts with angulation to the top of the

Fig. 64   A stop-cut
from quarte…

Fig. 65   …with
angulation.

attacker's wrist, stepping backward, clear of the attacker's blade.

4. As before, but this time the attacker steps forward, presenting for an angulated attack to flank; the defender moves to seconde. Instead of maintaining the parry, the fencer counter-attacks. He stop-cuts with angulation to under the attacker's wrist, using the back of the blade, stepping backward, clear of the attacker's blade. A stop-cut like this would be difficult to see with judges. The same stop-cut may be initiated by coming on guard in seconde, or deliberately attacking short, returning to seconde and stop-cutting as the opponent moves forward.

5. As before, but this time the attacker steps forward, presenting for a lunge to right cheek; the defender moves to prime. Instead of maintaining the parry, the fencer counter-attacks. He stop-cuts to the inside of the attacker's wrist, stepping backward, clear of the attacker's blade.

Having mastered these variations, try stop-cutting twice in succession. Depending on the speed of the attacker, you may need to take extra steps. A modern stop-cut in the midst of a fight is shown in Fig. 66.

The success of parries, once determined by judges who looked for contact with the blade, is now determined by lights on an electric box and by a blade which need not be presented only with its cutting edge.

Parries

Unlike foil and épée, sabre parries are actions which successfully block or deflect an attack. It would be a mistake to try to block a feint. The thumb is positioned behind the blade, opposing the direction of the cut. The blade is angulated away from the target, ensuring that the attacker's blade ends up on the guard of the defender.

When parrying tierce, the hand can move backward and forward, up and down, depending on the depth and angle of the attack. In *The Fencer's Companion*, Léon Bertrand shows subsidiary positions of low tierce and low quarte, termed *terza bassa* and *quarta bassa* respectively.

When parrying prime, form an arch so that you can look at your opponent beneath your sword hand. If you parry prime too low, you can hit your opponent's guard and lose the riposte.

The height of the parry of quinte (with judges) was generally on or about the forehead, but this was due to the use of the flèche – a flèche attack might be angulated, with a cut to head, at the last minute, going clean over the parry. With electronic scoring and the removal of the flèche, or cross-step, in theory this height can be lowered, but many high-calibre fencers parry higher to avoid a whipping blade (*see* Fig. 67).

Quinte may be taken from every guard.

1. The defender begins in tierce, at step and lunge distance to head. The attacker steps forward and lunges with a cut to head. The

Fig. 66   A stop-cut on the preparation.

Fig. 67 The sabre parry of quinte.

defender parries quinte, the guard moving in a vertical plane, and immediately ripostes to head.

2. The defender begins in quarte, distance as before. The attacker steps forward and lunges with a cut to head. The defender parries quinte, with the guard moving diagonally, and immediately ripostes to head.

3. The defender begins in seconde, distance as before. The attacker steps forward and lunges with a cut to head. The defender parries quinte, the guard moving backward and upward, and immediately ripostes to head.

4. The defender begins in prime, distance as before. The attacker steps forward and lunges with a cut to head. The defender parries quinte, the guard moving in a vertical plane, and immediately ripostes to head.

When parrying quinte at 'steam' sabre we tended to add a 'loop' when moving up from tierce to quinte in order to gather the opponent's blade. Istvàn Lukovich in *Fencing, the Modern International Style* describes this action as a 'semicircular parry', with the point moving downward and outward, travelling in a semicircular path. It should be pointed out that it was not unusual for the defender's hand to be further forward in those days

Consider the following:

5. The fencers begin at step and lunge distance to head. The attacker steps forward, does disengagement under the blade and lunges with a cut to head. The defender loops to quinte to gather the blade, immediately parries and ripostes to head. The attacker's blade is in the

inside of the defender's; without the loop, the attack would pass beneath the parry.

6. Distance as before, but as the attacker does disengagement under the blade, the defender begins to loop; on seeing the exposed underside of the attacker's wrist they perform a stop-cut, parry of quinte and riposte. The use of the loop prepares the way for the stop-cut, putting the blade in a forward position. The additions of a parry and riposte, or step back parry and riposte, against a deep attack take the ambiguity out of the stop-cut. This is also a safety shot if the stop-cut is unsuccessful.

When the guard is moving in a vertical plane (no loop), the parry of quinte is a fraction faster, as favoured by aficionados of modern sabre.

At sabre, a strong parry of quarte, with imme-

Fig. 68   The sesta parry.

diate riposte to head, can be difficult to parry and counter-riposte. Here are two options:

1. The attacker steps forward and lunges to chest. The defender parries quarte, late, immediately riposting to head. Given the close proximity and speed of response, it is difficult for the original attacker to get under the blade to parry quinte. One option is to reverse quinte, by lifting the parry on the defender's left-hand side, counter-riposting to flank. This is sometimes referred to as the 'sesta' parry, also known as the sabre parry of sixte (*see* Fig. 68). Alternative ripostes from here might be a through-cut to stomach or a delicate little cut to inside wrist. G.V. Hett in *Fencing* describes the parry of sixte as being usually formed following an attack parried in quarte, with riposte to head, the recovery to form the parry of quinte being difficult. Sixte protects the head from a vertical cut. In this case, the hilt of the weapon is facing inside and it is as if the hand were moved directly from quarte to parry the cut to head. It is, however, a clumsy parry. Léon Bertrand in *The Fencer's Companion* refers to quarte and sesta as secondary parries. Bac H. Tau in *Fencing Volume Four, The Sabre* simply refers to this traditional sabre fencing position as 'sixte'.

2. Attacks as before, the defender parries quarte, with immediate riposte to head; but this time the original attacker parries with high quarte and counter-ripostes to head. The counter-riposte descends from above the opponent's eyeline. The parry is taken with the hand a little forward and lifted, which positions the blade not far from the defender's mask. The riposte is made by quickly turning the wrist and using the fingers. With high quarte, the blade position is identical to the quarte, but the weapon is held higher, at about left shoulder level. Low quarte is about left thigh level.

Other parries may be usefully taken high or low, for example tierce or seconde. With high tierce, the guard is about level with the right shoulder;

with low tierce, it is level with the right thigh. High seconde covers the flank, but can vary in height. Rotating the wrist from quinte to high seconde is a good defence against a compound attack of head–wrist, or a sudden renewal to wrist, following a successful parry of quinte. Low seconde is at about thigh level, a good defence against a low angulated cut to flank.

At times, parries may be taken with the hand forward, by half-parrying. Albert Manley, in *Complete Fencing*, explains how the extended box for half-parrying may lead to wider or narrower parry positions, depending on how far out the parry is taken. A half-parry can be used in response to feints, waiting to determine the final line. At long range, an attacker may only reach your wrist and a full parry would be unnecessary and wasteful. A successful forward parry to quinte will touch the attacker's blade earlier, riposting with the blade well forward. It should be noted, however, that with modern electrical scoring a riposte from quinte to head is unlikely to register over an instantaneous renewal of the attack, an immediate riposte to flank being preferred. The defensive box in sabre is usually characterized by a two-dimensional shape formed by the defensive positions of tierce, quarte and quinte which form its sides. The true defensive box is three-dimensional, extending towards the opponent and taking the form of a pyramid on its side with the top removed. As the defender's hand moves forward, the area of the plane of the defensive box, being defended, reduces. Bert was taught the half parry under the term 'offensive–defensive parry'.

High quarte can be used as follows:

1. The attacker steps forward and lunges with a fast attack to left cheek. The defender parries with high quarte, the riposte is an immediate cut to head.
2. Against a left-hander, who feints to head then finishes the attack left cheek, initially parry quinte, then take a high parry of quarte, riposting as before. Although the left-hander has got inside your blade, high quarte is still capable of blocking the attacker's blade.

A high seconde parry, following quinte, leads to an easy point riposte.

1. The attacker steps forward with a feint to head, then lunges to flank. The defender parries successive parries quinte–high seconde. With the hand still in this elevated position, point facing forward, the point riposte is taken with relative ease. It should be remembered that at the time this type of defence was popular, sabreurs attacked with a rigid straight arm, first to head, then straight to flank – hence the success of the quinte–high seconde defence, rather than the more modern quinte–tierce. Useful against a flèche attack.
2. As before, but the attacker deceives the second parry and continues to head. The attacker may have to pull back the sword hand a little in order to achieve this last action, without touching the opponent's blade. The opponent stop-cuts under the wrist from the high seconde position, the blade already in position. There is a tendency for an attacker to break the timing on the third action of a compound attack, opening the way for the stop-cut. From high seconde, a parry of quarte is easy; from low seconde, this is more laborious.
3. As before, but the attacker deceives the second parry and continues to wrist. From high seconde the defender parries circular seconde and ripostes with point.

The point can also be used in other ways.

Use of the Point

The use of the point at sabre was always a clean hit. All hand actions at sabre begin with the point, which means using the fingers. A thrust with the point is made by the attacker extending the arm, with the hand in full pronation, the thumb at 9 o'clock; the blade is at right angles to the defender's target, the guard protecting the knuckles.

In a classical fencing bout, a fencer might feint with the point, deceive a parry, and cut to wrist. Against a flèche attack, the point could be extended to draw a single or double dérobement, used to slow the fight down.

Try the following:

1. The fencer begins in the on guard position, at step and lunge distance to target; the hand and blade are forward, point towards the target. The attacker goes for the blade, twice, moving forward. The fencer deceives the blade both times, placing the point lightly on the target. The attacker, attempting to take the blade twice, in his own timing, makes this an 'open eyes' routine – the fencer starts with no prior knowledge of how the timing of the double dérobement will happen, relying on reflexes to avoid the blade and make the correct ending.

2. This time, the fencer begins in seconde, at step and lunge distance to target; he steps forward and straightens the sword arm, as before. The attacker goes for the blade twice moving forward. The fencer deceives the blade both times, placing the point lightly on target. The act of stepping forward and straightening the sword arm switches on your concentration. The emphasis is on use of the fingers. Work at the speed that gives you 100 per cent success, no matter how slow.

3. Next, the previous exercise can be performed in any order from every known position: prime, seconde, tierce, quarte, quinte.

4. The fencer begins in seconde and must evade all the opponent's blade movements by moving the sword hand from seconde to tierce, quinte, prime, quarte, and finishing with a tierce riposte with the point, ensuring that all the guards are formed correctly.

5. Next, the opponent holds the sabre in the left hand and repeats 4.

This final version was favoured by Alf Simmonds, 'ever the showman'.

6. The opponent holds a sabre in either hand; he begins with the right-handed version of evading the blade, goes immediately into the left-handed version, finishing with a final flourish of tierce riposte point from the opponent's left hand, followed immediately by a quarte riposte point from the right hand.

Lewis Smith, formerly of Heriot-Watt University, was one of the few people to be taught this version by Bert. Lewis and I both got our fencing Blues at 'The Watt'.

With the introduction of electric scoring and the abolition of the off-target, fencers no longer rely on judges to see the hits land. Responding to this, the traditional role of the cut to flank has come full circle.

Angulated Cut to Flank

Traditionally, the cut to flank – like cut to right cheek – could be seen by judges. In the mid-1950s, the judging at competitions was good, the fencing not too fast and the piste 24m long. To solve the problem of hits landing on the off-target leg, fencers were taught to angle the flank attack upwards, under the defender's guard (*see* Fig. 69). If the blade landed off- and on-target at the same time, the hit was allowed. The parry of tierce is ineffective against such an attack, the only real defence being seconde.

In *Fencing (Foil, Épée, Sabre)*, priced 2/6 in old money (two shillings and six pence), originally published in 1952 by the AFA, the piste for épée and sabre is shown as 24m, with a warning line 2m from the end, and for foil as 12m long with a warning line 1m from the end. The referee, known then as a 'president', would stop the fencers at the warning line to warn that they were approaching the end of the piste. This book is a well-written introduction to fencing, with a foreword by Charles de Beaumont, prepared under the guidance of Roger Crosnier.

With the removal of the off-target, the same angulated attack still works, reaching below tierce, proving the necessity of seconde in the modern game. These days, a good flank attack can begin angulating below the guard, drawing seconde and opening up the upper arm, allowing the attacker to subtly change line by simply lifting the sword hand.

Many will feel that with the advent of electric scoring at sabre, where the lightest touch records a hit, the through cut is no longer required. Yet, in training, the skills derived from through cutting can be a valuable preparation.

Fig. 69　An angulated cut to flank.

Through Cuts

The through cut to chest is carried out with the arm extended, only breaking the wrist; it creates a small cutting action, drawing the flat of the blade through, then returning to the same point. The accuracy of this will dramatically improve if you look towards the left shoulder while applying the through cut. There is no initial rotation of the wrist to present the cutting edge, but the through cut is achieved by the wrist describing a small loop; the sword arm follows the wrist. This should be only as sufficiently firm as to come through cleanly, and not heavily applied. It differs greatly from a dry cut to chest, done with the front cutting edge of the blade.

When practising repetitive through cuts, it is advisable to use a training plastron. Although normally purchased from a manufacturer, these days a pattern for making your own training plastron can be found in Bob Anderson's *Improve your Fencing*.

1. First, at straight arm distance to chest, three short through cuts are performed slowly, in succession: right to left, left to right, right to left. The cuts begin below the shoulder and start by angling down a little towards the flank.

2. Next, at lunge distance to body, the attacker lunges with angulated attack to flank. The defender parries seconde and ripostes with a neat through cut to chest. The attacker continues to other lines, drawing parries of tierce, quarte, prime and quinte, all with through cut ripostes to chest. Eventually, this exercise can be done moving backward and forward, until the through cut to chest becomes near perfect.

3. This is perhaps a once-in-a-lifetime stroke. The attacker lunges with angulated attack to flank. The defender parries seconde, ripostes with reverse through cut – a short action, rising from right flank to left shoulder.

4. The attacker lunges to flank. The defender parries tierce, ripostes with through cut to chest, then does an immediate redoublement to flank with forward cut. There is no pause between the riposte and redoublement. Not all ripostes land.

5. As before, the defender parries tierce, ripostes with through cut to chest, which misses then continues with cut to flank, making this a compound riposte.

6. As before, the defender ripostes from tierce, misses, and continues to flank with a lunge as the attacker returns to guard. The original attacker stop-cuts to wrist, parries tierce, ripostes to head. The key to getting the stop-cut right is to return to guard with the hand well forward.

7. As before. This time the defender ripostes with a successful through cut to chest and immediate redoublement to flank, then steps back with the point extended. He performs dérobement as the original attacker attempts to take the blade. A good way to slow the fight down. Again, this shows the importance of keeping the hand well forward when returning to guard.

8. The attacker steps forward, lunges with feint to head; when the defender parries quinte, he completes the compound attack with through cut to chest. If the attacker misses the through cut, he stop-cuts with back edge of the blade on return to guard and steps back. The stop-cut may be performed as simple or compound (i.e. with a disengagement and forward cut to wrist).

9. The fencers begin at step and lunge distance to head. One presents the point in line. The attacker moves forward, attempting to take the blade. The opponent deceives with double dérobement, finishes with back cut to inside wrist then point to chest. A poor fencer does a dérobement from the shoulder, moving the sword arm around too much. Practised properly using the fingers, it prevents the fencer from getting a rigid hand. If the dérobement is done badly, the referee may say that the point was not in line with the target.

Having introduced renewals of the attacks, following through cuts, we will look at some typical renewals in a little more detail.

Remises/Redoublements

Although the word 'remise' is used to describe the actions which follow, the reader may prefer to think of these as 'redoublements' because the blade is moved to a different line. The important thing is the actions themselves.

1. The defender offers an opening to head; the attacker begins in tierce, steps forward and lunges, with cut to head; the defender parries quinte successfully and pauses briefly. The original attacker rotates the sword hand and remises to wrist, still on the lunge. The original defender continues slowly riposting to head; the original attacker rotates the blade under the wrist and cuts inside wrist with a second remise, returning to guard. When I first tried this, I found myself withdrawing my hand instinctively on return to guard, following the first remise.
2. As before, but the attacker begins in seconde, after the cut to inside wrist, returns to guard and steps back. The addition of the step back provides more realism.
3. The defender offers an opening to flank; the attacker begins in tierce, steps forward, rotates the wrist and lunges with cut to flank; the defender parries tierce successfully. The original attacker does remise, to the underside of the wrist. The original defender continues with riposte to chest. The original attacker rotates the blade under the wrist, cuts inside wrist with a second remise, returns to guard, parries quarte and ripostes to head.

The purists among you will no doubt be more comfortable referring to these remises as redoublements.

Continuity hitting puts you in touch with your body's natural rhythms and builds confidence; these skills are also a good preparation.

Continuity Hitting

Continuity hitting, sometimes called rhythm exercises, is a traditional approach which helps to loosen the wrist and sword arm, and develops confidence in the use of the various guards and cuts around the target. In the training exercises which follow, one fencer will take the part of coach and the other pupil.

1. At straight arm distance to body, the coach attacks repeatedly to flank, drawing successive rhythmic tierce ripostes to flank, right cheek, head, left cheek and chest; then the pupil returns to tierce.
2. Next, the coach attacks repeatedly to flank, as before, drawing successive tierce ripostes, to flank, right cheek, head, left cheek, through cut to chest, redoublement with forward cut to flank, redoublement to wrist – then parries tierce with riposte to head. The through cut is taken from the left shoulder blade diagonally to flank, leaving the blade in an ideal position for the redoublement to flank.
3. As before, the ripostes are taken rhythmically to flank, etc., concluding with the through cut to chest, redoublement with forward cut to flank. The coach then threatens different parts of the target, requiring the pupil to do an appropriate cut to wrist, parry and riposte.
4. As before, but the pupil does a lunge with the final riposte into any opening. For example, quarte riposte to flank, with a lunge, as the coach parries quinte and moves back. This introduces an open eyes response.
5. All of the above can be performed from tierce, quarte, seconde, prime and quinte.

Exercises like these help to develop rhythm and concentration. The objective is to make the sabre a part of you.

Four tierce ripostes:

1. The coach attacks repeatedly to flank, drawing successive tierce ripostes, providing different openings for the ripostes, sometimes changing the distance – riposting to flank, then flank–head with a lunge, returning to guard; riposting to head, then head–flank with a lunge, returning to guard. Traditionally, an exercise like this could be done incorporating a flèche.

Five parries and ripostes:

2. The coach attacks various parts of the target, to draw the following parries and ripostes in succession: seconde–right cheek, tierce–head, quinte–head, prime–head or flank, quarte–right cheek.

Ripostes with the point:

3. The coach attacks various parts of the target to draw the following parries, with direct or indirect ripostes, in quick succession: seconde – direct riposte to chest with point; circular seconde – indirect riposte with disengagement to chest with point; tierce – direct riposte to chest with point; circular tierce – indirect riposte with disengagement to chest with point; quinte – direct riposte to chest with point; circular quinte – indirect riposte with disengagement to chest with point; prime – direct riposte to chest with point; circular prime – indirect riposte with disengagement to chest with point; quarte – direct riposte to chest with point; circular quarte – indirect riposte with disengagement to chest with point.

4. As for 3, but a lunge is added to every indirect riposte, followed by a return to guard.

Having lessons like this every week used to be an important part of a sabreur's training. It gave a terrific feeling of completeness, and still does.
  More continuity hitting:

1. The coach attacks different parts of the target, drawing various parries, ripostes and redoublements. The pupil parries seconde, riposte right cheek, redoublement with through cut to chest, redoublement with forward cut to flank. The coach goes for flank, so the stop-cut is outside wrist, with return to tierce.

2. The pupil parries tierce; riposte head, redoublement with through cut to chest, redoublement with forward cut to flank. The coach goes for head, so the stop-cut is under the wrist, with return to quinte.

3. The pupil parries quinte; riposte head, redoublement with through cut to chest, redoublement with forward cut to flank. The coach goes towards chest, so the stop-cut is to inside wrist, with return to quarte.

4. The pupil parries quarte; riposte head, redoublement with through cut to chest, redoublement with forward cut to flank. The coach lifts the sword hand, requiring stop-cut under the wrist, presenting the blade to left cheek. The pupil ends up in prime.

5. The pupil parries prime; riposte head, redoublement with through cut to chest, redoublement with forward cut to flank, then immediately stop-cuts to inside wrist. The pupil returns to quarte. The coach attacks head–flank as the pupil steps back, parries tierce and ripostes to head.

Bert taught me this, wearing a half-plastron; the through cuts were adjusted to fit into the reduced area. It would be better to use a full-size plastron and protective sleeve if you wish to practise repetitive hits in this way.
  More continuity hitting:

1. The coach attacks different parts of the target, drawing various parries and ripostes with through cuts to chest: seconde, tierce, quinte, prime, quarte. The pupil returns to guard.

2. As for 1, but this time the redoublement to flank is added, followed by a choice of stop-cut, parry riposte. Against a cut to flank, stop-cut outside wrist, parry tierce–head. Against an angulated cut to flank, stop-cut outside wrist, parry seconde–right cheek. Against an attack to head, stop-cut under wrist, parry quinte–head. Against an attack to chest, stop-cut inside wrist, parry quarte–cheek or head.

This time, all the coach has to do is rotate his hand.

1. The coach rotates his hand, inviting cuts to wrist: outside, inside, under.
2. Then rotates in the other direction: inside, outside, under.

Fig. 70   Each
action…

Fig. 71   …
follows the…

73

Fig. 72 ...
next...

3. A fourth cut to the top of the wrist may be added to 1 and 2 if you feel ambitious.

Lastly, we will try a circular beat on the front of the blade, rotating to a back cut under the wrist, which can be developed into a rhythm lesson.

1. The coach extends his blade. The pupil practises using a rising circular beat on the front of the blade, finishing with a back cut under the wrist. The pupil's sword hand moves back towards the body, circling under the guard in one continuous movement. If the cut misses, this can revert to a direct cut to top wrist, which might be construed as a compound riposte.
2. As before, but after the successful back cut under the wrist, the pupil continues to cut top wrist, then does a circular beat on back of the blade and cuts to top wrist.
3. In conclusion, as for 2 but, following the circular beat on the back of the blade, the pupil lunges with a cut to head as the coach steps back.

The illustrations which follow have been improvised and simply serve to demonstrate the fluidity and rhythmic nature of continuity hitting exercises (*see* Figs 70–78).

Sabre is perhaps the easiest weapon to learn, but if you have a flaw it is easy for your opponent to take advantage of it. The weapon which most retains its original character is the épée, which we will consider next.

Fig. 73 ...
flowing.

Fig. 74 Speed
is not
essential...

Fig. 75 ...
but...

Fig. 76 ...
precision...

Fig. 77 ...
and rhythm...

Fig. 78 ...
are all
important.

Fig. 79   British Championships, Sheffield, 2008, Men's Individual Sabre. Chris Buxton (right) in the air, and Tom Mottershead (left). (Photo: Graham Morrison)

3 Épée

Introduction

One of the more interesting books that have come along in recent years about modern electric épée fencing is Johan Harmenberg *et al*'s *Epee 2.0: The Birth of a New Fencing Paradigm*, developed from the thoughts of progressive coach Eric Sollee, who simply asked if it was possible for a fencer with lower technical ability a) to control the technical level of a bout; b) to control the distance in a bout; or c) to force his opponent to fence in his own area of expertise, rather than the opponent's. Here, the emphasis is primarily on winning; style is secondary.

For the classical stylist, Imre Vass's *Epee Fencing:*

Fig. 80   Senior World Championship, Paris, 2010. Men's Team Épée Final, Ulrich Robeiri, France (right), and Cody Mattern, USA (left). USA led for two-thirds of the match, but France eventually won. (Photo: Graham Morrison)

A Complete System offers an alternative approach. It is based on the proposition that foil technique provides the necessary technical basis for épée, with new elements gradually introduced, and as such is perhaps more evocative of a time when a master might prefer his pupil to lose elegantly, in a gentlemanly fashion, rather than win at the risk of using bad technique, and of a time when judges had to determine whether or not the application of the épée point had been successful or not.

Many types of point have been used during of the evolution of the 'steam' épée, broadly termed '*pointe d'arrêt*'. The specification for the lengths of these early points can be found in Julio Martinez Castello's *The Theory and Practice of Fencing*. The early épée points bit into the jackets, sometimes drawing a little blood in the form of triple pinpricks; modern electric épées are a delight by comparison.

Épée fencers may indeed base their movements and actions on what they did at foil, then adapt them in a way that is beneficial for épée; this transition can happen very quickly.

The Grip

Holding an épée French grip is similar to foil. The grip must be held firmly, in order to control the opponent's blade. An alternative to this is holding the grip close to the pommel, which extends the fencer's reach by a few centimetres – particularly advantageous for a fencer whose game is dérobement. This tends to be too weak against fencers who constantly attack the blade and makes

it difficult to manipulate the blade, particularly when parrying; also, the extended target is more exposed. Another variation is where the index finger rests flat along the side of the handle, with the thumb lying on top. This may help in making angulated attacks to the opponent's wrist, but provides a poor grip, which is easily disarmed by a heavy beat. An orthopaedic grip is easy to hold firmly and allows for careful control of the épée.

Transition from Foil to Épée

How does a coach spot the potential épéeist? Generally, you can observe two types of reaction in young foil fencers. If you stick your arm forward, some tend to parry, others will counter-attack. The ones prone to stop-hitting tend to become épéeists. When a foilist wants to try épée for the first time, a coach may not have much time before the first fight and therefore should emphasize the following: renewals, opposition and counter-attacks (*see* Fig. 81).

What follows is an amalgam of ideas from a number of coaches. Doing it this way will get someone fencing simple épée fairly quickly and should help to produce an épéeist who does not simply pick at the wrist.

1. The coach provides an opening suitable for an attack to body; the pupil lunges and hits lightly to body. Sometimes the coach steps back, giving a choice reaction, for a renewal of the attack to forearm with a tiny movement

Fig. 81 Counter-attacks are commonplace at épée.

forward, allowing the hit to land. This is done in two movements. Many new épécists will start off by practising one movement and then stop.

2. The coach offers an opening to the upper wrist/forearm by dropping the point; the pupil straightens and hits (no lunge). The coach lifts the point. The pupil gathers the blade through circular sixte and time-hits to body, by straightening his sword arm as the coach moves forward. This is pure opposition. An épéeist's point is his first line of defence.

3. As before, but as the pupil gathers the blade through circular sixte, the coach steps back and the pupil lunges to body.

4. The coach attacks to leg, the pupil stop-hits to wrist, hitting just above the guard as the coach's hand moves forward. The coach lifts the blade, the pupil then lunges with blade opposition to body.

5. Finally, the coach places the tip of the épée above the pupil's guard, moving forward. The pupil parries through circular sixte, straightening the sword arm at the same time; the coach continues moving forward. This is a stop-hit with opposition to body. The coach returns pressure on the pupil's blade, steps back; the pupil disengages and lunges with opposition on the blade and redoublement to body. The coach drops his point a little when the pupil lunges with opposition. The three factors mentioned earlier – renewals, opposition and counter-attacks – are all present: principally, a counter-attack with opposition and renewal with opposition.

If foilists are about to try épée for the first time, it is unlikely that you would start by teaching them octave. At this point they will not be used to the heavier weapon; the sword hand will tend to drop in octave, losing control of the blade and leaving them vulnerable to a low-high attack. They can, however, be taught a stop-hit threat to foot, or to slow an opponent down by feinting to the mask.

Fig. 82   Line up the point first...

The hit at épée is quite distinctive and must be done in a particular way in order to develop accuracy.

The Hit
Bert first coached épée with Roger Crosnier's *Fencing with the Épée* in one hand and an épée in the other. Foil and sabre came easy to him, but he realized early on that he would have to make a greater effort at épée. This is particularly evident when we examine the level of care that he applies to the application of the hit.

The point is aimed with the fingers. After the hit, relax the hand to release the tension in the blade. For the purposes of the training exercise that follows, one fencer will be referred to as coach and the other pupil. When training with repetitive hits to wrist/arm, always use a training sleeve.

Fig. 83   ...then extend and hit.

1. The coach opens up a little, moving the sword hand towards sixte and exposing the inside wrist. The pupil lines up the point first (*see* Fig. 82) with a tiny movement of the sword hand, then extends the point to hit (*see* Fig. 83). The coach's opening may begin with a 4-inch (100mm) movement of the sword hand and then reduce it to 2 inches (50mm). There are two distinct actions in the extension of the hand: the lining up of the point, then the hit proper. Many épéeists try to make the hit in one complete action, but if their opponent steps in they can miss the wrist. Using this method, the hit still lands. Done carefully, you should never miss at this distance.

2. The coach now offers a small opening on top, right, left and below the guard, varying the order. The pupil lines up the point with a tiny movement of the sword hand and extends the point each time to hit. There are four different types of alignment, each requiring a slight angulation to suit, using the thumb and forefinger. Practised properly, the hits should land 100 per cent of the time, the pupil's confidence increasing with this success. This is an open eyes lesson, as the pupil does not know which of the four openings to expect next and the coach's timings may vary.

An épéeist who warms up with a fight before a competition may lose, thinking that if he did not do too well in the warm-up fight, he will not do well in the competition. The fight had perhaps been less than perfect and did not build his confidence. Warming up with this training routine as an alternative, however, leaves the fencer feeling that he should be 100 per cent successful with the hit from the start.

3. The coach steps back. The pupil steps forward. On the landing of the pupil's back foot, the coach offers one of the four small openings, as before. The pupil lines up the hit, introducing a lunge as the coach draws out the distance. This tiny initial alignment makes all the difference.

Next, a second hit (redoublement) is added.

4. The pupil attacks the wrist, as before; an immediate redoublement is offered by the coach on the return to guard. The redoublement is performed by the pupil with a straight arm as the coach's hand is moving forward, with the point offering no immediate threat. In time, several redoublements can be offered after hits to the four target areas, requiring continuous concentration by the pupil, who must not retract his sword hand until all the hits have been made. This is open eyes training. If the coach goes for the leg or foot, this can become a rassamblement.

Charles de Beaumont, in *Fencing*, describes how the rassamblement is made: bringing the front foot back to the rear foot, while straightening the legs, the body drawn back in an arc.

5. The pupil attacks to wrist, as before – this time performing remise, as the coach releases the blade, followed by redoublement with disengagement on return to guard, again maintaining a straight arm. The redoublement with disengage may also be applied, taking the blade.

In épée, the return to guard can be an offensive action. If a fencer returns to guard with the hand held back, this can be termed 'defensive'; if the arm is left out, it is termed 'offensive'. The first line of defence is the point; if you miss, you will often be hit.

If a fencer is concerned about getting hit on the wrist by an accurate opponent, his sword hand will move backward or forward.

6. The coach offers an opening to wrist. The pupil lines up first and then extends the point to wrist and lunges. The coach does nothing. The pupil returns to guard.

7. As before, but after the hit the coach reacts, quickly extending the sword hand forward as the pupil returns to guard. The pupil does prise-de-fer on the coach's blade and lunges.

8. As before, but after the hit the coach reacts, suddenly taking the sword hand back. The pupil immediately steps and lunges to body. This can also be done by launching a flèche, if the distance is correct. Another option is to lunge initially to wrist, then flèche from the lunge position, with the retraction of the hand.

The flèche may be effectively deployed when the distance to be covered is greater than a lunge: effectively, between lunge and step and lunge distance. The speed of the flèche depends on the angle of inclination of the body: usually between 45 and 60 degrees. The greater the inclination, the more the fencer has to chase to regain his balance (*see* Fig. 84) and the more effective is the impulse in the front leg in pushing forward – the hit lands before the back foot, moving forward, hits the ground to regain balance (*see* Fig. 85). At épée the flècheur may be vulnerable to counterattack, risking a double hit (*see* Fig. 86). Generally, the flèche should not be taught to beginners. An advanced fencer should be trained to relax the grip as the hit lands, to minimize the risk of breaking the blade. At épée, the fencer may hit twice when executing the flèche – the first hit on the flèche itself, the second immediately after, while passing the opponent.

Imre Vass in *Épée Fencing: A Complete System* describes the flèche from lunge as particularly useful in relation to renewed attacks. In

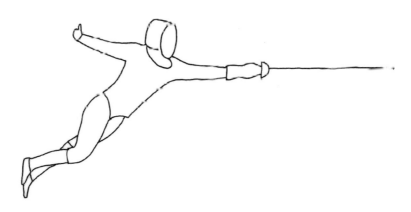

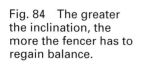

Fig. 84 The greater the inclination, the more the fencer has to regain balance.

Fig. 85   The hit lands before the back foot follows through.

the lunge position, the fencer leans forward, pushing his centre of gravity past the front foot, requiring considerable strength and athletic ability. When leaning forward, the fencer can withdraw his front foot about one foot (300mm), making the transition easier. Additionally, the forward lean can be further assisted by a short appel-like step of the rear foot. Bert recalls that Julian Tyson, formerly of Aberdeen University, was particularly adept at this type of manoeuvre. I later came across Julian's name again as he compiled the index for Edmund Gray's *Modern*

British Fencing 1964–1981 and appeared in the photographs of Tom Norcross's *Fencing: The Foil.*

With épée, the unconventional character of the weapon means that renewals of attacks are more important than with conventional weapons like sabre or foil. All the above actions can be made later, with opposition and at longer distance.

In the previous exercises, we had the option of going for four target areas around the wrist, in any order, including more than once in the same

Fig. 86   The flècheur may be vulnerable to counter-attack, risking a double hit.

spot. These can be done standing still, with lunge, step and lunge and on return to guard, giving many combinations. For maximum benefit, it is essential to maintain a classical on guard position throughout, with point above or below the opponent's guard.

Whilst the mask is a valid target, a gentleman does not, as a rule, hit it, although feinting towards the mask may discourage an opponent from moving forward.

An important topic, sometimes overlooked in épée, is the return to guard.

Return to Guard

A common fault with young masters, when teaching épée, is their belief that the hit finishes the phrase. Returning a pupil to guard, in a covered position, is how the top masters do it.

1. The coach opens up a little, moving the sword hand towards sixte and exposing his inside wrist. The pupil lunges to hit inside wrist. The action being completed, the pupil simply returns to guard in his own time. The hit finishes the phrase.
2. Now, a better approach. The coach begins as before, this time returning the pupil to guard, covered, in relation to the coach's blade presentation. This can be done with any known covered position.
3. This begins as before, the pupil returns to guard, either with the arm bent, or sometimes leaving the sword arm straight. This is done randomly and is intended to leave the opponent unsure of what will happen next. A wrong anticipation of the return to guard, with a bent arm when the sword arm is left straight, may lead to being caught unawares by the straight arm when stepping in. Mistakenly going for the blade, expecting a straight arm, may lead to a redoublement on the arm. The simplicity of this lesson is that anyone can do it, at any level.
4. The coach opens up a little, on top of the wrist. The pupil lunges to hit top wrist, this time returning to guard with the point angled inwards, next to the 5 o'clock position on the coach's guard. This is designed to restrict

the opponent's options, since moving the sword hand forward can lead to a hit on your hand. In a duel, placing the point next to the hand in this way prevents your opponent from moving forward without first taking the blade.

5. Next the coach opens up a little, on top of the wrist. The pupil lunges to hit, but is successfully parried in sixte. The coach applies pressure to the blade. The pupil does redoublement with disengagement to inside wrist, followed by a redoublement under arm, followed by a time-thrust, through circular sixte, as the coach moves forward. Hits made with opposition are at the very heart of advanced épée fencing.
6. As before, but after the coach's successful parry of sixte, the pupil leaves the point out, executing a remise as the coach releases the blade, which is followed by redoublement with disengagement to inside arm. On returning to guard, with a straight arm, the pupil hits under the hand, followed by a circular time-thrust through sixte as the coach moves forward. Finally, the coach lifts his blade and returns the pupil to guard, in a covered position. Training like this ensures perfect balance.
7. A lot of attacks are false at épée. The pupil lunges with a false attack to top of wrist, which is parried in sixte. The pupil returns to guard, lifting the sword hand to head height, angling down to top wrist at an acute angle, using the opponent's guard as a gun sight. Dragging the point in this way makes it virtually impossible for the opponent to gather or beat the blade. If the hit misses, the pupil does a lightning redoublement to mask, landing only on the rim of the mask, never where the face is.
8. Previously we used a high hand; now we will use a low hand. The pupil lunges to top wrist, which is parried in sixte. The pupil returns to guard, this time crouching low, angling the point up at an acute angle, to hit below the wrist. I messed this up on my first attempt by trying to squat down while still on the lunge.

9. A more speedy response is achieved when the pupil lunges to hit top wrist, is parried in sixte, then returns to guard in octave, immediately whipping the point up below the wrist as the coach's hand moves forward, then gathering the blade immediately with hit to top shoulder. Because this stop-hit is so fast, many épéeists will take their hand back, creating the opportunity for a flèche attack. If the hand goes back, a direct flèche is possible; if the hand moves forward, take prise-de-fer to top shoulder, through circular sixte. This is second intention.

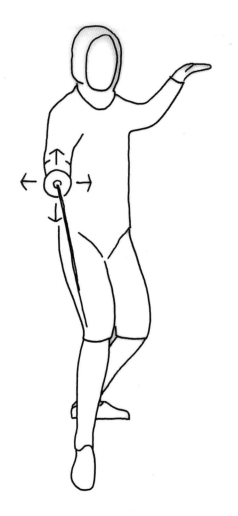

Fig. 86   The cone of defence.

A unique part of the épéeist's defence system is the use of the guard to protect the forward target, which follows next.

The Cone of Defence

Broadly speaking, defence at épée is similar to foil, but the guard also tends to be used, which is sometimes referred to as the 'cone of defence' (*see* Fig. 87).

The fencers carrying out this training routine will be referred to as coach and pupil.

1. The coach holds the point in his left hand, then presents the blade randomly in four positions: above the guard, below, outside and inside (*see* Figs 88–91). Each time, the pupil deflects the point away, moving the guard up, down, and side to side. Holding the point ensures that it does not drift out with the movements of the guard.
2. As before, but after each deflection, the coach places the point on the forearm as a riposte, still holding on to the blade. The three ripostes from upward and side to side movements of the guard are all with opposition on the blade. The riposte from the downward movement of the guard is with detachment.
3. As for 2. The coach continues to hold on to the blade, moving backward and forward as required. The hits are delivered first with a half lunge, then a full lunge, followed by a return to guard.

Parries on the right side – like sixte and octave where the hand does not move across, exposing the forward target – are particularly useful at épée.

Circular Sixte

The circular parry of sixte forms a fundamental part of the épéeist's defence.

To practise circular sixte, try the following:

1. The attacker places the tip of the épée a little past and above the defender's guard, the point projecting approximately 2 inches (50mm). The defender slowly practises circular sixte, using mainly the fingers, and ripostes to top arm. Épée is heavier than foil and the

Fig. 88   Above the
guard...

Fig. 89   ...below...

Fig. 90   …outside…

Fig. 91   …and inside.

blade tends to drift out a little before the riposte is made.

2. As before, but this time the defender moves the sword hand over 1 inch (25mm) in sixte, takes circular sixte and ripostes to top arm. The hand is now in the correct position to take the circular parry and the riposte is quicker. Another way is to move the hand forward a little, but this leaves the defender open to redoublement.

This explains the fundamental difference between circular sixte at épée and foil. If your hand is in the correct position at épée from the start, all you have to do is move your hand forward for the riposte and you will have more time to get opposition on your opponent's blade.

3. The attacker goes a little deeper. The defender moves the sword hand over 1 inch (25mm) in sixte, in preparation for making the circular parry of sixte. This time, the circular parry is taken a little further back, making way for an immediate prise-de-fer riposte to leg or foot. The additional leverage, gained by moving the hand back a little, assists in the prise-de-fer.

4. The attacker places the tip of the épée a little past and above the defender's guard, projecting approximately 2 inches (50mm). The defender takes circular sixte, as before, but moves the sword hand forward with the parry, straightening the sword arm at the same time and making a thrusting riposte with opposition.

5. The attacker presents the tip of the épée, as before. The defender lifts the sword hand with the circular parry and does an angulated opposition riposte to inside arm.

6. Next, the defender drops the sword hand with the circular sixte parry, does an angulated opposition riposte to inside arm, which is at a difficult angle to parry.

7. The defender provides an opening to top wrist. The attacker lunges to top wrist, which is parried in sixte. The defender lifts his sword hand, allowing the original attacker redoublement below the hand. Still on the lunge, the original attacker places the point in the 5 o'clock position, next to the opponent's guard. With the arm still straight, he performs a circular sixte time-thrust to upper arm as the original defender moves forward. After the redoublement, the original defender lowers his sword hand to cover, making way for the time-thrust. In the 5 o'clock position, if the original defender attempts to take the blade, which cannot easily be done, the original attacker will deceive the blade with redoublement as there is plenty of room for manoeuvre. The circular sixte time-thrust can revert to the shoulder, the area around the shoulder/upper arm being one of the most vulnerable parts of the épée target. Even if the time-thrust is deceived, it still has a good chance of hit-ting as it becomes a stop-hit into disengagement.

8. As before, the attacker places the tip of the épée a little past and above the defender's guard. The defender takes circular sixte, rotating the wrist sharply into tierce and riposting suddenly with opposition to body. The riposte from tierce (Italian school) is awesome. The wrist turns as the hand is moving forward, giving a horizontal bend in the blade as the point lands. The whip on the blade makes it very difficult to stop. The riposte is virtually always to body.

9. Every now and then, the attacker simulates a surprise flèche attack to body. The defender takes circular sixte, but keeps the sword arm bent, angulating the riposte into the attacker's body. The defender is taken by surprise and may have to take a small step back when taking the circular parry. When training, the simulation of the flèche need not be fast; the defender should maintain balance and riposte with precision.

Circular sixte is probably the most important parry at épée. At foil the parry of quarte has a similar importance. Some épéeists use a system of parries in defence, which can be very effective. One distinguished British international used the sequence sixte, circular sixte, octave, circular octave, very effectively.

As with circular sixte, the use of octave at épée is different from foil.

Octave

Foilists coming to épée are less used to parrying octave, which is of necessity taken lower to protect the leg/foot. The riposte is achieved by lifting the hand up a little, through sixte; opposition ripostes will also need the hand to move slightly forward.

1. The attacker lunges to hit just under the wrist. The defender parries with a semi-circular parry of octave and carries the blade round to complete the circle, riposting with opposition to upper arm. If the attacker deceives the parry, the defender continues into a circular parry of octave, finishing as before.

Always responding to low-line attacks with octave can make a fencer predictable and vulnerable.

2. The attacker lunges to high-line, perhaps shoulder. The defender takes the blade suddenly with a 'U'-shaped parry of octave (a 'U' shape on its side); gathering the blade, he culminates with the sword hand on octave, riposting to body. From here, the defender can riposte with the sword hand high or low. A riposte like this, following a surprise taking of the blade, has great power: effective against flèche attacks.

3. The attacker lunges to high-line – upper arm or shoulder (*see* Fig. 92). The defender parries octave by first lifting the point quite high, describing an elliptical or oval-shaped movement of the point (the longest dimen-

Fig. 92   The point is presented in the high-line.

Fig. 93   The defender parries octave, by describing an elliptical arc...

sion being up and down) as it continues to octave (*see* Fig. 93). This keeps the point in the sixte line. At the lowest part of the ellipse, the point is positioned over the opponent's leg, thus opening up the lower target for a quick, natural riposte; the hit can also be directed to foot (*see* Fig. 94). Although a narrow elliptical action, the emphasis is on an up and down movement of the sword hand. This can be done starting in sixte or octave. If the attacker manages to deceive the elliptical parry, the original defender

can make a beautiful stop hit under the original attacker's hand, which is still high.

In choosing between a circular and elliptical octave, a fencer may wish to consider the following:

4. The attacker lunges just above the wrist. The defender parries with a circular parry of octave, which is sufficient to clear the point. He carries the blade round again, riposting with opposition to upper arm. This circular

parry takes the point out of line, making a hit to the leg more difficult.

5. The attacker lunges to high-line – upper arm or shoulder. The defender parries with an oval-shaped parry of octave, riposting to leg or foot. A circular parry of octave will not work effectively on an attack this high. More hits, proportionately, are made to the zone outlined by the upper arm/shoulder than anywhere else.

I saw Bert teach the oval parry of octave to a relative beginner. The beginner hit leg first time. In Britain, we do not use the leg hit enough. Épéeists often train in tracksuit bottoms, which would make a leg hit impracticable. We should concentrate more on how to hit the leg.

The Leg

British masters in the middle of the twentieth century taught that you should hit the foot, but not the leg. The background to this was that foil, épée and sabre were taught together, and it may have been difficult to put on leg protection when moving from one weapon to the other. Not so with Maître Cottard of Paris Racing Club, whose épée fencing lessons involved the whole body.

Fig. 93 …placing the point over the opponent's leg.

1. The coach moves the épée as a fencer. When the point goes up, or out, the pupil attacks to leg. We start with these blade openings.
2. The coach stands on guard, at a distance where an attack to leg is not possible. When ready, the pupil moves forward 1 foot (300mm) and attacks to leg, which is now at the correct distance. Now we have added the choice of distance.
3. The coach stands on guard as before; the pupil threatens to leg. The coach attempts a stop-hit to wrist. The pupil parries and ripostes to arm, which is second intention.
4. Lastly, add choice reaction using 1, 2 and 3.

The leg is a great place to hit with a compound attack. For best effect, your opponent's point should be moving away from the target as the hit lands.

5. The pupil aims to top shoulder, the sword arm a little bent, on the feint, so it can be straightened to full extent on the second part of the compound attack to leg. The emphasis here is on point speed, which in épée can be forceful.
6. The pupil steps forward, threatening inside wrist. The coach's response is to draw back his sword hand. The pupil finishes the compound attack to leg. This is an ideal time to go for the leg.
7. The coach attacks on the quarte side. The pupil parries quarte and ripostes with croisé to leg.
8. The coach lunges to top wrist. The pupil parries circular sixte and binds to leg. This is particularly useful when done with a lunge on the opponent's return to guard. Quarte and sixte binds are both useful for leg hits.
9. The coach attacks top shoulder. The pupil parries tierce and drops the point suddenly down to leg, with opposition.
10. The pupil attacks to upper wrist. The coach parries circular sixte. The pupil immediately does a redoublement to leg. This is particularly effective if the defender's hand has moved back with the circular sixte.
11. The pupil attacks to upper wrist. The coach parries circular sixte. The pupil immediately does a redoublement, with bind to leg.

By hitting the leg consistently, you can affect your opponent's balance.

Ideally, you want to take hold of the blade when going for a leg hit. To do this, you must learn how to 'feel' the blade, gradually building up your self confidence so that you can do this under fight conditions.

The following exercises are designed to achieve this.

1. The coach extends his blade. The pupil gathers the blade, anti-clockwise, through quarte: first to hit inside arm, round again to hit upper leg, round again to hit foot, then round again to hit inside arm. This is first done in situ (standing still). The pupil must keep the blade in contact at all times, ensuring a smooth transition.
2. As before, but next the pupil takes the blade round to hit inside arm; round again to hit upper leg; round again to hit foot with a lunge; round again to hit inside arm recovering backwards; round again to inside arm; round again to hit upper leg; round again to hit foot with a lunge; round again to hit inside arm, recovering backwards. The coach must adjust distance to allow for the two lunges and the inside arm hits when recovering to guard.
3. As for 2, but the pupil finishes to inside arm, after recovering forward.
4. As for 2, but finishing with flèche to body.

The advanced fencing techniques listed here for foil, sabre and épée may be practised by coach and pupil, or simply by fencers meeting in a club. The role of the coach is quite unique in fencing and will be examined next.

Fig. 95   Senior World Championships, Paris, 2010, Men's Team Épee. Geze Imre, Hungary (right), and Pavel Sukhov, Russia (left). (Photo: Graham Morrison)

OPPOSITE: Fig. 96   Senior World Championships, Paris, 2010, Women's Individual Foil L/32. Katja Waechter (right) and Martina Emanuel (left). Waechter won the fight. (Photo: Graham Morrison)

PART II
Advanced Coaching Techniques

4   Coaching/Lessons

Introduction

In coaching, both group and individual forms of instruction are required. László Szabó's *Fencing and the Master* is a definitive study of the role of coach and pupil and is much to be admired. Lesser known is H.T. (Bert) Bracewell's *Advanced Foil Coaching*, which concentrates on individual lessons. This was based on an Inverclyde course (August 1976), the objective of which was to build

individual lessons geared to the needs of top fencers who already know the strokes, but need to be able to use these actions in competitive situations. In this, the applications of new strokes are incorporated into the fencer's existing game and don't just take over the lesson completely; this is still, in many ways, the true testing ground of a coach.

Notes on Individual Coaching

When giving a strict 'Crosnier' classical lesson to an advanced pupil, getting on top of a tricky technical situation can give the pupil a strong psychological lift. Finish a lesson like this – doing something that your pupil is comfortable with and does best – will leave him on a 'high note'. Remember that the pupil before you has done you the honour of learning from you; this honour is returned by giving your experience and skills.

In a fifteen-minute individual lesson there is:

- A period of about one minute at the beginning and end where you are getting ready, or finishing.
- Three to four minutes' warm-up. This is required to attune the pupil to what follows.
- Three minutes' run-down.
- This leaves a learning period of five or six minutes. New material should be presented early, while the pupil is still fresh.

In a thirty-minute lesson:

- The beginning, end, warm-up and run-down are the same.
- This leaves a period of twenty or twenty-one minutes for learning.

Fig. 97   Bert Bracewell and pupil.

The value of the learning period in a thirty-minute lesson is worth at least three fifteen-minute lessons.

A coach's standard will drop if coaching only beginners. A good supply of coaches is needed at a basic level for beginners, as needs arise. An improving coach becomes like an opponent, changing distance and timing in response to the pupil. It is then up to the advanced pupil to work it all out.

In trying to pass coaching exams, it is helpful to have a formula for success.

Coaching Formula

A simple formula for passing a coaching exam on a defensive subject follows next. For the purposes of demonstration, we will look at successive parries, but this formula could also be used for other defensive topics. It can apply to any weapon.

1. Start by teaching successive parries in situ (standing still). Do not proceed to the next stage until the pupil has demonstrated the required skills and has a good understanding of the topic. Ensure that the riposte lands correctly on target.
2. Next, teach successive parries with a step back. This is required because of the speed of the attack. Ensure that the pupil's foot and hand co-ordinations are correct and that they do not snatch the blade.
3. Open up the distance. The pupil is attacked on the preparation (step forward) with a compound attack, then takes successive parries and ripostes.
4. Do any of 1, 2 and 3, and riposte with a lunge.
5. The pupil attacks with a lunge, short of the target, then returns to guard. The coach attacks with a compound attack. The pupil takes successive parries and ripostes.
6. The pupil attacks with a lunge, which is parried. The coach does a compound riposte. The pupil takes successive parries and ripostes, still on the lunge.
7. Against the coach's first feint into the high-line of the compound attack, the pupil takes the following premeditated responses: circular parry – simple parry, simple parry – circular parry, circular parry – semicircular parry. Ensure that the first parry is always taken absolutely correctly.
8. Next, do successive parries at different speeds (i.e. slow first parry, faster second parry).
9. Due to the depth of the attack, ensure that opposition is used on some ripostes. If close, angulation, or even opposition and angulation, may be deployed.

With slight variations to the strokes, this formula could be used for other defensive topics: parries and ripostes, counter-ripostes, beat parries, counter-time, etc.

With experience, various types of lessons emerge.

Types of Lessons

Giving various types of individual lessons stops the coach from getting bored; also they provide a repertoire of techniques that can be appreciated by the pupil. What follows are some alternatives:

- A classical lesson, based on the teachings of Roger Crosnier. Do an action properly, for the sake of being a good fencer, with a love of the sport – not necessarily winning, but being part of a team.
- An 'open eyes' lesson. A simple description being 'no blade contact' (i.e. dérobement, simple or compound), deceiving any parry, with target selection (high or low).
- A choice reaction lesson. The pupil gathers the blade, ending the stroke according to what happens (i.e. no response, fast simple attack; pressure response, attack by disengagement; as the pupil tries to gather the blade, the coach attacks on the preparation, the pupil does parry and riposte).
- Lessons using various specific moves. Look at the many variations already listed under foil, sabre and épée.
- A fighting lesson. The coach sets up situations and the pupil responds (i.e. the coach straightens his arm and the pupil uses various beats or prises-de-fer).
- A close quarters lesson. The pupil learns to continue fencing at close quarters.

- A tactical lesson. Use of the piste.
- A preparatory lesson for competition. A hard lesson before matches or competitions, stopping when the coach feels that the pupil's attitude and point are correct.

The examples that follow are at foil.

Classical Lesson

It is important that the coach's pressure, openings and the pupil's responses are small. This kind of work is based on Roger Crosnier's *Fencing with the Foil*, as taught by Alf Simmonds.

1. The coach begins by providing the smallest of openings. The pupil does a neat, precise straight thrust. Great emphasis is made on economy of effort.
2. The pupil applies the lightest of pressures to the coach's blade. The coach reciprocates, with a return pressure; the pupil disengages, lunging to target. The disengagement, a tiny 'V'-shaped action, just clears the blade, which only slightly bends with the hit.
3. Next, the pupil returns to guard and parries quarte, with immediate direct riposte. The quarte parry is the smallest parry imaginable; the riposte immediate, following light contact with the blade.
4. The pupil takes the tiniest circular parry of sixte, with direct riposte. It is the neatness of the parry which gives the riposte speed. For the tiny circular sixte parry to work, the pupil needs to move the sword hand over 1 inch (25mm) after the parry and then riposte.

A great deal of effort in this lesson goes into the coach's use of distance. Now with tiny movements of his blade, the coach moves in from far away.

5. The pupil parries quarte, indirectly ripostes with disengagement; then parries sixte, indirect ripostes with disengagement; then parries octave, indirectly ripostes with disengagement; then parries septime, indirectly ripostes with disengagement (this can be around the guard, to the low-line). If the point goes around the guard, this is disengagement. This sequence makes a good continuity hitting exercise. A lot more time is spent developing hand and foot co-ordination with this type of lesson, as well as the occasional use of the lunge. For example: lunge followed by backward recovery, lunge followed by forward recovery, parry and riposte on the lunge, any combination of indirect ripostes; this creates much better balance while doing indirect ripostes. In the middle of a lesson, Alf used to ask the pupil to perform a set piece (say doublé dégagé, doublé de doublé, or coupé dessous). It would be the pupil's responsibility to determine the correct distance, making sure that you do what your brain tells you is physically perfect. Alf would call out a stroke and do his part to perfection. In this way, he taught the fencer to win on crucial hits, with fantastic technique and control of distance; the later hits in a fight are often decisive. He might slip in close, suddenly offering quarte riposte with disengagement, hitting the pupil if he is not at the correct distance.

6. Next, the pupil envelopes the blade and, on the coach's release, launches a beat attack. Normally, envelopment dominates the top of the blade. Here, it is taken with a slightly bent arm, allowing the beat attack to be possible. If the pupil's arm was straight, the beat would land on the forte of the coach's blade, which might be given as a parry. With the arm slightly bent, the beat is much clearer. The onus is on the pupil to get the correct distance, not the coach. This can be developed into a very advanced lesson, aimed at the later stages of a bout with time running out when, given an opportunity, you strike to win.

Historically, fencing bouts had not been subjected to time limits, until at a master's championship in the 1930s the bout lasted seven hours.

'Open Eyes' Lesson

Open eyes may be defined as without any contact with the blade.

1. Coach and pupil begin at straight arm distance to target. The pupil straightens his sword arm,

the coach attempts to take the blade, the pupil avoids the blade, without touching; the coach leans forward a little for the point to land.

2. Next, at half-lunge distance to target, the pupil straightens his sword arm, avoiding the coach's blade; the coach leans forward a little for the point to land. If the pupil's blade is touched, this may not be sufficient to displace the point away from the target: simply move the sword hand out 1 inch (25mm) and continue as before.

3. The pupil lunges short, then returns to guard, with the sword arm still straight. The coach moves forward, attempting to take the blade. The pupil performs dérobement.

4. The pupil does a full lunge, lunging just short of the target, then avoids the coach's blade, without touching; the coach leans forward a little for the point to land. This is not a redoublement, since the blade has not been parried; there is no meeting of the blades.

You are now able to make a continuity hitting exercise out of 1, 2, 3 and 4.

5. The pupil lunges short and then recovers forward. This is a good time to launch a flèche, after avoiding the coach's blade.

Observation of your opponent is key to this. You have to study your opponent to determine what might happen next. Many fencers do not use their eyes properly.

With gradual training, the pupil gains confidence. Then suddenly, the coach puts in a fast one, getting the pupil to go compound, requiring observation on the pupil's part. The coach goes hard and fast, attempting to take the blade, but must pause briefly between the two hand movements in order to gain the desired effect.

With open eyes, target selection is kept simple, usually between high- and low-lines. A beat direct can be performed, when the coach's blade is presented correctly. This may develop into beat-pause as the coach goes for the blade, the pupil performing disengagement; or beat, attack high, lunge low, as the coach goes for the blade.

Choice Reaction Lesson

Coaches will argue at length about the difference between 'choice reaction' and 'open eyes'. Definitions presented in this book are that working off the blade is 'choice reaction'; 'open eyes' is where the blade is not found. As with most things in fencing, these distinctions, applied in words, are probably less important than the actions themselves.

Of necessity, the following is kept very simple:

1. The pupil changes engagement from sixte to quarte. If the coach does not react, the attack continues, with lunge direct to high-line. If the coach reacts by returning the pressure, the pupil disengages and continues with lunge indirect to high-line. If the coach reacts by return pressure but raises his sword hand a little, the pupil disengages continuing with a lunge to the low-line. Hence, we have target selection. When the coach raises the sword hand a little, his sword hand may come down suddenly to octave, making a compound low-high attack possible by the pupil.

2. The pupil does a bigger change of engagement, from sixte to quarte, which can be deceived. The coach avoids the blade and attacks with counter-disengagement; the pupil does a parry riposte. I instinctively parried sixte, but a circular quarte parry would have been better. Not all fencers can do counter-disengagement, followed by a second counter-disengagement.

The most important part of a choice reaction lesson is the correct use of distance. A tactic at the end of the piste might be to lunge short if the opponent goes for the blade, do dérobement, or let the opponent touch the blade and react.

In choice reaction, you have to have something to react against. Doing a really bad change of engagement from sixte to quarte invites a counter-attack on the preparation by counter-disengagement, which you can then parry and riposte.

The most important part of a change of engagement is that the point leads, ensuring that the blade is collected; if the guard leads, this is easily deceived. The attacker can improve his chances of collecting the blade by applying a tiny pressure to the defender's blade before attempting the change. The opponent tends to react against this pressure, making it more difficult to deceive the change of engagement.

Vary the lines in change of engagement, and a choice reaction might be to parry quarte, sixte or octave.

It is in the mentality of the fencer to experiment. If a fencer's blade is taken twice in succession by a change of engagement from sixte to quarte, he will invariably launch his counter-disengagement on the third attempt. Fencers at Latista Fencing Club, Alf Simmonds' club, were taught to change their parry on number three. A fencer who does disengagement and draws a parry of quarte does not believe his eyes, so does it again, launching his one-two attack on the third attempt. If you spot an opening, go on number two.

Every fencer has a favourite stroke. Why is it his favourite stroke? Because he gets lots of hits with it! If you lose a hit, you must change to avoid being hit again with the same stroke.

3. The pupil lunges and is parried. If there is no riposte, he does redoublement. If there is a riposte, he counter-ripostes.
4. The pupil straightens his sword arm. The coach does envelopment. The pupil responds with ceding, or opposition parry and riposte. If the envelopment is not well executed, the blade can be slipped early on, leading to a hit. This is particularly useful at épée.

Fighting Lesson

In this lesson, the coach adopts a much more positive fencing position, setting conditions for the pupil; it is a role-playing situation. The pupil must keep distance. A fighting lesson does not last long: four to five minutes is enough, then rest and do it again. The coach needs to rest. A four-minute lesson is probably ideal, because it prepares the pupil for full concentration in a three-minute bout. The coach may simulate situations that have been observed at competitions. It is helpful if a coach can attend competitions to watch his fencers.

A fighting lesson is a transition between lessons and competitive fencing.

1. The coach attacks suddenly, drawing quarte riposte from the pupil with detachment, and remises immediately, making a loud noise to signify that he considers that it is his hit. The pupil has to learn to use a croisé, a classical prise-de-fer response. In a fight, the referee may not be able to determine if the point was cleared from the target by the parry. To remove doubt, the pupil ensures that only one hit lands.
2. The coach does a very slick beat on the pupil's almost straight arm blade. It is not possible for the pupil to disengage under the beat. The pupil then briefly disengages, lunging short and returning to guard in octave; then he presents the blade with a straight arm, 3 inches (75mm) further out. The coach attempts to beat the pupil's blade. The pupil now deceives successfully, because this is a much larger movement.
3. The coach goes for the blade. The pupil avoids the blade with disengagement and lunges. The coach steps back. The pupil solves this problem by doing a forward reprise.
4. The coach goes for the blade. The pupil avoids the blade with disengagement and lunges short, returning to guard immediately. As the coach moves forward, he does a parry riposte, or beat-parry riposte. The pupil launches a false attack, to see what the coach will do. The coach does the same response two or three times until the pupil responds correctly, solving the problem. As the lesson progresses, the coach might do a circular parry two or three times to draw a doublé; or parry quarte, to which the pupil might counter-riposte.
5. The coach comes on guard too close to the pupil and hits immediately. This is one of the oldest tricks in the book. The pupil must learn to keep perfect distance. While the pupil is resting, the coach moves 1½ feet (450mm) closer: the pupil must return to good fencing measure immediately (*see* Figs 98–100). The coach also works at different speeds and the pupil must adjust, without verbal correction.

6. The coach does a lunge, the pupil steps back and then does nothing. When the attack continues, the pupil parry ripostes. Think of the step back as an offensive action to draw the attack.

Fig. 98   The coach moves too close to the pupil.

Fig. 99   The pupil must return to good fencing measure...

Fig.100   ...From where he may launch a successful attack.

At all times, the lesson must be technically correct and the distance varied. The pupil should concentrate on waiting for the best time to launch an attack and then return to a correct on guard position, ready to attack or defend. If the pupil makes a mistake, he should be hit, or otherwise made to realize what can happen.

Also, every time the pupil attacks, the coach can stop-hit, side-step or duck.

Close Quarters Lesson

A small fencer will have to get inside the distance of a taller fencer. In order to continue fencing when you get in close, the guards do not touch. The last thing you want to do is step back, as this looks very negative to the referee: in the event of two hits landing, the hit may be given against you.

The exercise which follows begins with the economical parry of quarte, mentioned earlier. You can turn the wrist in supination to fix the point from all the positions described.

Imagine a situation where the opponent is attacking at three distances: normal lunge distance to body, closer, then at close quarters. As the opponent moves closer, he can angulate around your blade with increasing effectiveness. Your parry should respond to this. To be successful, you will find that your sword hand rotates a little more each time, the point swinging out, but the hand does not move back.

Imagine next that the attacker's sword hand can be presented at three different heights: with a straight arm and the blade parallel to the floor; next, with the sword hand a little higher; then a little lower. This may be because an opponent is a little taller or smaller, or simply looking for a weak spot in your defences.

What I have described are three hand heights and three distances, making a total of nine possible blade positions for an attack, each of which requires a suitable parry of quarte.

What follows is a training simulation. Imagine the attacker is moving forward, closing distance, without which there would be no justification for rotating hand and blade. This is a reaction against an opponent who moves forward, leading the way to a high parry of quarte, with riposte to the upper part of the back; or a low parry of quarte, also with riposte to the lower part of the back.

1. The pupil begins by placing the point on the coach's plastron and leaving it there. The coach extends his point on the quarte side. The pupil parries, with an economic parry of quarte (*see* Fig. 101), ripostes back to exactly the same spot on the coach's plastron and leaves it there.
2. Next, the pupil rotates his hand a little, in quarte, lifting the point with the blade at 45 degrees to the horizontal (*see* Fig. 102) and then ripostes, as before.

Fig. 101 Begin with an economic parry of quarte.

Fig. 102 Next, the sword hand is rotated, with the blade at 45 degrees...

Fig. 103 ...then rotated a little further, with the blade at 80 degrees.

spot. Supination of the hand will make the hits neater.

Other routines follow:

1. The pupil and coach are in sixte, with blades crossed and at close quarters. The pupil moves along the blade, angles the point, hitting with opposition without letting go of the blade – very much like an old-fashioned froissement, displacing the coach's blade with a sharp, strong grazing action, forward and downwards, from foible to forte. The pupil is being trained to place the point on target and not to panic, jab, or jump back uncovered, rather to dominate the blade, using angulation to place the hit on target.

Fig. 104 The sword hand is raised a little higher in quarte...

3. Then the pupil rotates his hand a little further, in quarte, lifting the point with the blade at 80 degrees to the horizontal (*see* Fig. 103) and then ripostes, as before.
4. 1, 2 and 3 are carried out carefully in rhythmic succession.
5. The coach extends his point, as before, but lifting the sword hand a little higher. The pupil reciprocates by lifting his hand a little in quarte, repeating 1, 2 and 3 (*see* Figs 104–106).
6. The coach extends his point, dropping the sword hand a little lower. The pupil reciprocates by dropping his hand a little in quarte and repeats 1, 2 and 3.

Do all nine parries and ripostes, slowly to start with, always trying to hit precisely the same

2. The pupil and coach are in sixte, with blades crossed and at close quarters. The pupil does

Fig. 105 ...then rotated, with the blade at 45 degrees...

Fig. 106 ...then rotated a little further, with the blade at 80 degrees.

a cutover; this is especially effective if the coach drops the point in prime, which many fencers do at close quarters. The secret is to ensure that only one light goes on, otherwise this can be ambiguous.

3. The next is a form of open eyes training. The pupil stands on guard at close quarters. The coach does not hold a foil, attempting to touch the pupil's blade only with his gloved hand. The pupil avoids the hand, placing the point on the target, with sword arm still bent. If there is no movement by the coach, the pupil simply hits. If the coach moves continuously, the pupil hits successfully, again and again, with renewals.

4. The pupil parries quarte. The coach moves in so deep that it is hard for the pupil to place the point; now the coach's point is well past the pupil's target. The pupil does an angulated hit, on the sixte side, with bent arm.

The themes, so far, for our close quarters lessons have included opposition, angulation and renewals.

5. The pupil and coach are in sixte, with blades crossed and at close quarters. Holding on to the blade, the pupil makes three hits, with a bent arm, moving down the target. The hits land, first from sixte with the thumb at 1 o'clock, then 2 o'clock, then 3 o'clock, turning the wrist each time.

6. The pupil steps in close, engaging the coach's blade in octave, without forcing corps à corps and then concludes with a flying cutover from octave.

The coach can create a situation where close quarters fencing can take place in a lesson by stepping forward, lunging, or using a flèche (simulated). If the coach goes high, the pupil can go low and vice versa. The pupil's body movements play a greater role: effacing the trunk of the body, ducking, side-stepping and displacing the target away from the fencing line, which may prove more effective than a parry.

Tactical Lesson

The object of this type of lesson is to use the whole length of the piste, to observe your opponent and exploit tactically what you see are his strengths and weaknesses – also, to create situations that you might use to your advantage. You could begin by observing leading opponents at fencing competitions.

1. Coach and pupil begin at the on guard lines. 'On guard. Are you ready? Fence!' The pupil moves in quickly, taking the blade, trying to get the coach to lean back. Putting an opponent's weight on his back foot will tend to eliminate a surprise attack, since balance has to be restored before an attack can commence.

Typical observations of an opponent might involve:

2. The coach continually beats the pupil's blade. The pupil learns to come on guard in octave, which eliminates most beats.
3. The pupil is on guard in sixte. The coach does a coulé down the blade, followed by a flèche. The pupil learns to take circular quarte, cutting-the-line, sometimes called a contraction parry, and stepping back if the coach gets too close.
4. A fencer, returning from a competition, should have a debriefing session with his coach. If he lost, he will tell his coach what happened. The coach can then prepare a tactical lesson based on this.
5. Know your best strokes. Your coach can give you a tactical lesson based on these. Bert's favourite stroke is a one-two attack. To teach this, start with the pupil disengaging on the

coach's pressure. This is then parried by the coach. Next, the pupil does a counter-riposte, still on the lunge. Then, the pupil decides to do a very fast one-two attack.

Three strong themes discussed here are lessons based on: the coach's observations; a debriefing session; or, doing things that you are best at.

Preparation Lesson for Competition

It is very important to do a warm-up before a lesson, which should include the pupil using distance correctly and using his brain. In the second day of a competition, a fencer may be a little stiff and the coach will have to go slowly. The coach should finish on a high note, with a favourite stroke which he knows the pupil does well.

It is important that the coach knows who his pupil is fighting first, and whether he is right- or left-handed. A coach should be able to warm up a fencer using both hands. Bert used to try to find out which piste his pupil would be on and to warm him up near where he was going to fence in order to get used to the lighting.

1. The coach starts by giving an opening for a straight arm hit to target, then adds a step with the straight arm. Then, a simple parry (quarte), and riposte. He allows the pupil to choose when to do each action.
2. The coach applies pressure to the blade, adjusting the distance to get the pupil to lunge with disengagement. Initially, the coach makes his actions so big that the pupil can see them coming. Gradually, the coach tightens up.
3. Now, the coach begins to use the whole piste, changing the timings of these actions so that the fencer has to start looking for the blade. He introduces a series of slow counter-ripostes; although relatively slow, the pupil must hit every time.
4. By offering openings for high- and low-line, with a step forward and lunge, the coach introduces target selection, getting the pupil to use his eyes.
5. The coach offers a few stop-hits, introducing a 'check and change' mentality into the fencer

for the first fight; many first fights are lost if a fencer is not thinking yet.

6. Finish with a beat attack. The pupil has to choose the moment, only doing a beat when the blade is momentarily stationary. The coach is now beginning to move at different speeds. At no time has the fencer hit off-target. There is nothing complicated: a very simple series of moves.

A warm-up like this takes four or five minutes, leaving a gap of ten minutes before the fight. Putting a fencer straight on the piste after a warm-up does not work; also, there should be a short warm-up between rounds. An aspiring fencer should have his own coach available at a competition – someone who knows the fencer's physical, mental and technical abilities.

These are all typical individual lesson types. What follows next are others based on different approaches.

Silent Lesson
In the late 1960s when I was a novice coach under the SAFU coaching system, as part of our coaching exam we were required to give a four-minute lesson without speaking. Under this system, the assumption was that the coach giving this lesson was never wrong.

István Lukovich in *Fencing: The Modern International Style* refers to the need for silent lessons. Jules Campos, in *The Art of Fencing: Three Weapons, Foil, Épée, Sabre*, points out that silent lessons develop two essential qualities in the pupil: a sharp sense of observation and speed at reaching decisions. In Ziemowit Wojciechowski's *Theory, Methods and Exercises in Fencing* he refers to the idea of the silent lesson, where the trainer gives the fencer various signals and the task of the fencer is to develop logical responses. Bert has always acknowledged the fact that many of the ideas that he uses come from a variety of sources, but in the development of the silent lesson, over a number of years, he has made it very much his own.

George Sandor, the renowned épéeist who attended Edinburgh University, insisted that all key fencers in the club gave the following silent lesson to other fencers, prior to receiving a lesson from the coach. This was introduced to new fencers with terrific effect: although a small club at that time, all eleven represented Scotland at various levels.

The following actions at foil have many combinations; in these, a fellow fencer takes the part of the coach.

1. The coach takes the blade away, the pupil hits at straight arm distance to target, lightly bending the blade. The pupil must maintain the proper distance.

2. The coach steps forward and backward. The pupil keeps distance, continuing to hit at straight arm distance to target on the opening. The coach's openings and footwork must be smooth. The pupil must vary his speed, as appropriate, to match the movements of the coach.

3. Next, the coach introduces lunge distance by stepping back. He gives an opening, requiring the pupil to straighten his sword arm and lunge. The pupil returns to guard after each hit. He steps back with an opening, requiring the pupil to step forward, with the straightening of his sword arm, then lunge. He steps forward and then gives an opening, requiring the pupil to step back, straighten his sword arm and then lunge. He steps forward with an opening, requiring the pupil to straighten his sword arm at straight arm distance to target; after which, the coach reintroduces lunge distance by stepping back. The pupil now hits with a straight arm/straight thrust at various distances.

4. A very quick second opening can be introduced as the pupil returns to guard, to encourage a very fast second lunge – catching the pupil unawares, forcing him to speed up and change the timing.

5. The coach covers a fencing line, with blade contact; when pressure is applied, the pupil disengages. As in 3, this is applied at various distances.

6. At lunge distance, the coach gives an opening. The pupil lunges and the coach steps back to avoid being hit; the pupil now has to do a forward reprise.

7. The coach gives an opening for the pupil to attack with a lunge. On the pupil's return to guard, he quickly steps back with an opening, requiring a fast step forward and lunge. The pupil must react quickly to the change in pace.

8. The coach moves forward and backward, varying the speed; the pupil follows. This time, the coach closes the line, requiring disengagement, or offers an opening. This introduces choice reaction and sentiment du fer.

9. Now, the coach suddenly uses simple attacks. The pupil must parry and riposte, using quarte and sixte randomly. This is mixed with all the previous actions, requiring careful rhythm in foot and hand control by the coach. Speed is not essential. Technique is fundamental.

10. As before, but the coach covers and the pupil must disengage with the riposte.

11. Now, as the coach returns to guard, the pupil must lunge with the riposte.

12. The coach closes the line or offers an opening, drawing a simple attack, which he parries; the pupil does a counter-riposte, still on the lunge.

13. As before; but when the coach's parry is drawn, the pupil does a one-two.

14. On the coach's change of engagement, the pupil does a counter-disengagement. It should be observed that the pupil has been under constant pressure to respond throughout.

15. On the coach straightening his sword arm, the pupil does a sudden beat attack with lunge. The coach can add a stop back first, then straighten the sword arm, inducing a step forward beat attack with lunge. All the above actions should be mixed.

16. As a final gift to the tired pupil, you can speak. Ask the pupil to offer a straight arm pointing to target. As the coach attempts to take the blade, the pupil will carry out a dérobement. The coach's footwork must always be rhythmic and the blade presentations clear and crisp.

This type of training was introduced in Scottish fencing, before the Polish 'open eyes' approach was introduced in England, and attempts to respond to genuine fight conditions.

Lesson with a Mixture of Actions

A number of top international coaches give foil lessons like this:

1. On an opening, the pupil lunges. The coach may attempt to take the blade in sixte and quarte sides, requiring the pupil to disengage with the lunge, introducing open eyes technique. Between each of these actions, the pupil must return to a near perfect on guard position. The lesson continues slowly.

2. The coach attacks the pupil in various ways, requiring the pupil to parry and riposte. The pupil must be perfectly covered. The coach may introduce additional parries and ripostes – say, quarte riposte, twice in succession.

3. The pupil finds the blade and then instigates a one-two attack. At advanced level, the coach may wish to deceive the pupil's attempt to take the blade, requiring the pupil to do a second intention parry and riposte.

4. The pupil straightens his sword arm and performs a dérobement, deliberately slowing the fight down. The coach sometimes finds the blade, possibly with prise-de-fer. The pupil must respond with parry and riposte, sometimes incorporating a ceding parry.

5. Change the parry to circular sixte, following a simple attack from the coach – but only if the point is near the upper guard, otherwise quarte might be more appropriate. This lesson should still be very slow.

6. Moving backward and forward, the coach extends his blade; the pupil does a very fast beat attack.

7. The coach does a very slow walking attack. The pupil must use a series of different parries and ripostes. This might be necessary at the end of a crucial fencing bout.

This type of lesson can be developed in great detail, for all three weapons. Lessons based on a platform of seven actions will be demonstrated later, for foil, sabre and épée, the aim of which is to build a platform of ingrained actions for competitions.

Introducing Tactics into a Fencing Lesson

Producing more interesting and demanding lessons stops a coach from getting into a rut. The following foil lesson is based on four choices. The coach decides what these choices will be – they will not be the same for everybody.

1. The coach presents his blade, with hand forward. The pupil attacks, straight down the blade, like a coulé. If the coach does not react, the pupil completes the lunge high or low. If the coach reacts sharply to cover with the blade, the pupil immediately does disengagement high or low. This action is often masked in fencing.
2. The coach applies pressure to the pupil's blade. The pupil does disengagement and lunges. None of these attacks will be 100 per cent in depth, more like 80 per cent. If the coach lowers his hand, the pupil does disengagement, reaching to top shoulder. If the coach takes a parry, the pupil does parry counter-riposte. Care must be taken with the speed, position and width of this parry. The pupil can disengage close to the guard to see if the coach takes a circular parry. If so, does he riposte immediately, or pause? The pupil may counter-disengage around the circular parry, or allow the parry to take place successfully and then do a redoublement if there is a pause.
3. The coach offers the blade. The pupil beats the blade, to see what happens. If the coach straightens his arm, the pupil may take the blade or beat again. If the coach's hand moves, trying to parry, the pupil may disengage. The pupil can beat both sides of the blade, looking for weaknesses to exploit.
4. The coach provides an opening. The pupil attempts a one-two attack. The pupil is looking to see if the coach can parry two actions. If this appears to be a weakness, he may continue with the attack. Does the coach's

blade go sideways or forward? If successfully parried, the pupil may parry and counter-riposte. If the coach does not parry, the pupil may revert to low-line. If the coach parries quarte, followed by circular quarte, the pupil may need to find a counter-disengagement.

New pupils will be asked to write down their observations to help them train tactically. Another way of learning tactics is to observe an important fight in a competition, then discuss it with the coach. It is certainly a good way of productively involving the pupil in the content of lessons.

Rhythm Lesson

The following foil lessons should be performed rhythmically.

1. The pupil does a parry of circular sixte, riposte, which is parried by the coach; when the coach releases the blade, the pupil's remise lands. The same action can be performed also from quarte, octave and septime in succession and in any order. This is a good exercise for getting a fencer to use thumb and forefinger.
2. The pupil does a parry of circular sixte, riposte, which is parried by the coach; when the coach releases the blade, the pupil's remise lands. The pupil does a parry of circular sixte, riposte with disengagement, which is parried by the coach; when the coach releases the blade, the pupil's remise lands. The pupil does a parry of circular sixte, followed by one-two riposte; when the coach releases the blade, the pupil's remise lands. Lastly, the pupil does a parry of circular sixte, then a riposte with a doublé on a lunge, which is parried; when the coach releases the blade, the pupil's remise lands. This is a good lesson for getting the hand moving and the wrist supple. Rhythm is necessary for speed. To be successful, the coach must be in a balanced position all the time: you pay for a coach's hand and experience.

Rhythm lessons like these can improve not only the pupil's but also the coach's technique. Exercises may be practised in the on guard position, then with a lunge. To be successful, the coach must maintain a realistic depth of point at all times. When working effectively, footwork can be added.

1. The pupil does a parry of quarte, direct riposte; parry of quarte, indirect riposte with disengagement; parry of quarte, one-two compound riposte; parry of quarte, doublé riposte.
2. Now the coach must skilfully maintain distance. The pupil steps back, does a parry of quarte, riposte direct; parry of quarte, indirect riposte with disengagement and lunge; recovers forward, with a parry of quarte, one-two compound riposte, with a step and lunge; recovers backward, with a parry of quarte, flèche with doublé riposte.

Care and precision in the application of these skills is essential for a successful outcome, particularly when movement is introduced. When stepping back, the pupil completes the parry of quarte precisely when the front foot lands; this hit is true, because his feet are stationary, solid to the ground. The indirect riposte by the pupil will only be made when the coach gives a clean, lateral pressure on the blade, without anticipation, extending smoothly into a lunge as the coach steps back. With forward recovery, the parry is completed with the landing of the rear foot. A perfectly balanced forward return to guard prepares the way for the one-two compound riposte, which follows without hesitation: the step forward is short, the deception clean and lunge correct. When recovering forward, the sword hand should

not move back close to the body, compensating for the forward movement: if deceived in quarte, with the arm locked back, it would be impossible to take a second parry. For the pupil to flèche, the coach must keep distance like a fencer. Another quarte riposte may be added if required to make the pupil counter-riposte on the flèche.

The pupil learns to concentrate on footwork, blade work and timing, which in turn helps to build his confidence. At this level, it is often good to get the pupil to train with an electric foil, which has a different balance.

Avoiding the Coach's Unarmed Hand

The pupil extends his sword arm, pointing towards the coach's target. The coach attempts to touch the blade with his unarmed sword hand. The pupil avoids the hand, without his blade

Fig. 107   The coach attempts to touch the blade...

Fig.108   ...with his unarmed sword hand.

Fig.109   The pupil avoids the hand...

touching it, placing the point on the target and, if necessary, lunging. Later, as the pupil grows in confidence, both of the coach's hands may be used, attempting to touch the blade, which makes the exercise a little more difficult (*see* Figs 107–112).

This kind of training offers a number of distinct advantages: it develops finger control, ensuring that the pupil will miss the opponent's (off-target) sword arm, at foil; it helps to develop judgement of distance – later, with compound attacks, he will have the confidence to feint more deeply.

A compound attack and a dérobement can be practised using the same technique. A slight pause is necessary by the coach, to ensure that the pupil gets a straight arm before completing the compound attack; this is best done with a change of pace. With dérobement, the straight arm estab-

lishes priority, so long as it continuously threatens the opponent's target. The coach moves forward a little to allow the hit. Whilst a dérobement is perhaps best understood as an action in the high-line, the option to direct the blade to the low-line may also be applied.

At any stage, a weapon may be introduced into the sword hand, which works equally well for developing point control at foil and épée. This is an excellent exercise for two fencers when a coach is not available. It may be practised standing still, with a lunge, with steps forward and backward.

A lesson using these ideas might be developed as follows:

1. The coach and pupil stand at straight arm distance to target, at foil. The coach attempts

Fig. 110   ...without touching it.

Fig. 111   Later, both of the coach's hands may be used...

distance. All responses are with a lunge and the coach has to move in for the parry.

6. As for 5, but steps forward and backward are included with the lunge.

7. When the lunge is made, the coach steps backward. If the coach's foot moves forward, the pupil does a remise. It the coach touches the blade and moves forward, the pupil does a parry counter-riposte. If the coach goes for the blade, the pupil does a redoublement.

8. Lastly, if the coach goes for the blade, the pupil can do a one-two attack.

to touch the blade with his unarmed sword hand, the pupil neatly deceives the hand without it touching – each time, lightly placing the point on the target. The aim is to get the pupil's fingers moving.

2. The coach moves his sword hand forward. The pupil lightly touches the side of the hand, simulating a parry of quarte and riposte.

3. Or, the coach's hand is withdrawn and he moves back a little. The pupil steps forward and lightly hits the target.

4. Combine 1, 2 and 3. Learn to do the parry perfectly. The pupil must be careful not to hurt the coach by getting the distance wrong. The coach can fetch the left hand into play occasionally, searching for the blade to make the deceptions of the blade a little harder.

5. Now, 1, 2 and 3 are performed at increasing

Throughout this lesson, the pupil concentrates on looking where the guard is, which is the location of the coach's unarmed hand.

Fig.112 ...which makes the exercise more difficult.

Coaching Plastron with Two Red Lines

Bert observed a distinguished international coach giving a fencing lesson with two red lines on the front of his coaching plastron, just below the elbow. The coach referred to this as 'the area of indecision'.

1. From quarte, tierce, octave, etc. (all of the guards), the pupil lunges, hitting between the lines on the coach's plastron. These comprise: attacking from different guards, at different distances, with different hand positions (i.e. thumb in the 1o'clock, 3 o'clock, 9 o'clock positions, etc.), with deft use of thumb and finger co-ordination. Hitting between these lines poses specific problems for the coach: an accurate parry of quarte misses the blade; if octave is taken, a hit in the high-line can be achieved by the pupil, simply by turning the sword hand, a very fast attack. Even with successive parries, the coach's defence will be moving further than the pupil's point; the only real hope of a second parry is high septime or prime, although the coach will still be vulnerable under the arm. This is the dilemma for the defender when attacked in this way.

2. If the pupil provokes a successful parry of seconde by the coach, the blade can be lifted as before with instantaneous redoublement, which can also be achieved by blocking the coach's blade in opposition.

3. A feint between the red lines may draw a large circular sixte by the coach. The pupil's responses might be doublé, staying in the low-line with the hit landing between the red lines, or doublé, finishing in the high-line.

Fig. 113 Quarte...

Fig. 114 ...riposte, hitting between the red lines.

Fig. 115 Sixte...

4. Next, the pupil changes engagement from sixte to quarte, finishing with cutover to low-line and landing between the red lines.
5. A one-two attack can be launched by feinting between the red lines, finishing the compound attack in the same place.
6. Ripostes from quarte and sixte may be practised, always landing between the red lines (*see* Figs 113–116).
7. A sudden beat attack, landing between the red lines, can be difficult to stop (*see* Figs 117–118).

These are good tactics for a smaller fencer to use. The aim would be to use this approach to get two hits in a fight, putting the defender at a disadvantage. When demonstrated to me, this lesson lasted twenty minutes, with the pupil always hitting between the red lines. The result was greater accuracy, with minimum hand action and maximum finger action.

Blade Preparations with a Variety of Footwork

The original version of this lesson was demonstrated to me at foil, but these general principles can be adapted to sabre and épée.

1. For foil, start at lunge distance to body. The pupil steps forward, engaging the blade with a light circular sixte action. He straightens the sword arm immediately as the rear foot lands, holding onto the blade securely with hit to chest – continuous and flowing. The

Fig. 116   ...riposte, hitting between the red lines.

Fig. 117   A beat attack...

pupil returns to guard at foil fencing measure. All the routines which follow should be practised sequentially, without stopping. Later, once the whole routine has been mastered, the timing may be varied. The pupil carries out all these routines in his own time – not rushing, but concentrating on good technique.

2. The pupil steps forward, engaging the blade with a light circular sixte action. This time he moves the feet close together so that the heels touch, and finishes with hit to chest, as before. He returns to guard at foil fencing measure. Exercises 1 and 2 prepare the way for 3 and 4, which will increase the distance.

3. The pupil steps forward, engaging the blade with a light circular sixte action. The coach steps back. The pupil straightens the sword arm, holding on to the blade, and lunges with hit to chest. Returns to guard.

4. The pupil steps forward, as before, this time moving the feet close together so that the heels touch. The coach takes a larger step back. The pupil proceeds as before, lunging with increased distance, with hit to chest. Returns to guard.

5. The pupil steps forward, as before. The coach does a counter-disengagement, straightening his sword arm, into the slow preparation. The pupil immediately parries quarte, with the sword hand well forward and then ripostes, with opposition, to chest. Returns to guard, with step back; resumes foil fencing measure. The purpose of the parry in this part of the sequence is to make way for the beat that will follow. Because of

Fig. 118   ...with lunge, hitting between the red lines.

the close proximity of the coach's point, it is safer to riposte holding on to the blade.

6. Start at step and lunge distance to body. The pupil steps forward, engaging the blade with a light circular sixte action. The coach does a counter-disengagement, straightening the sword arm, into the slow preparation. The pupil immediately does a beat attack, lunging to body, and returns to guard at lunge distance to body. To successfully launch a beat attack requires this additional distance.

7. Next is a repeat of 3. The pupil steps forward, engaging the blade with a light circular sixte action. The coach steps back. The pupil straightens the sword arm, holding on to the blade, then lunges with a hit to chest. Returns to guard.

8. The pupil steps forward, engaging the blade with a light circular sixte action. The coach steps back. The pupil quickly steps forward, firmly holding on to the blade, applying additional pressure. The coach steps back, immediately responding to the sudden change of pace. The pupil lunges fast with hit to chest. Returns to guard.

9. The pupil steps forward, as before. The coach steps back. The pupil steps forward quickly, moving the feet close together so that the heels touch, and firmly holding onto the blade. The coach takes a larger step back, immediately responding to the sudden change of pace. The pupil lunges fast with hit to chest. Returns to guard. There is considerable pressure, forcing the coach back, possibly off balance. Bringing the rear heel forward close to the front heel is sometimes referred to as 'gaining measure'. This can be useful if the opponent is out of distance, or is observed to habitually retreat when attacked.

10. The pupil steps forward, as before. The coach steps back twice. The pupil does a crossover step, then lunges to chest. Returns to guard.

11. The pupil steps forward, as before. The coach takes a large step back. The pupil does a flèche attack to chest. Returns to guard.

12. The pupil steps forward, as before. The coach steps back, then steps back again. The pupil does a sudden balestra, followed by a lunge to body, initiating a sudden change in pace. Returns to guard.

13. Begin at lunge distance to body. The coach begins to step forward. The pupil moves his rear foot back only, launching a sudden beat attack to body, attacking on the preparation. Returns to guard.

14. Begin at lunge distance to body. The pupil moves his front foot forward only and then launches a beat attack to body: a surprise beat.

115

Platform of Seven Foil Actions

At the 1990 World Championships in Lyon, Bert observed a number of world-class masters doing a similar kind of lesson. This involved a system of taking up to seven actions to a very high standard, each with, say, three variations, to build a platform of ingrained actions for competitions. On average, you would aim to get three of your five hits using this system. If you could get one more hit (perhaps by luck), then you would aim to finish with your best stroke. That was the theory. Each group of strokes would be tailored to the individual; for example, a smaller student might have more footwork introduced.

The coach tends to introduce variations which may follow on from observations; for example, a coach may wish to introduce variations in defence to improve a pupil's defensive responses.

A lesson like this is likely to take place after a brief warm-up. The coach moves forward and backward throughout the lesson, ensuring that the pupil is constantly on the move, keeping distance. The main core actions and optional variations might be as follows:

Main Core of Actions

1. When the blade is in the correct position, the pupil, whose own blade is kept low, engages the coach's blade and does a simple attack when he thinks this can be done successfully (*see* Figs 119–120).

Variations

a. If there is no response, the pupil continues with a straight thrust.
b. If there is an answering pressure on the blade, the pupil does disengagement with lunge.
c. If the coach attempts to change the line by rotating into quarte, the pupil does a counter-disengagement with lunge.
d. If the coach takes the blade away so that an engagement is not possible, the pupil continues to move forward and backward, keeping distance.

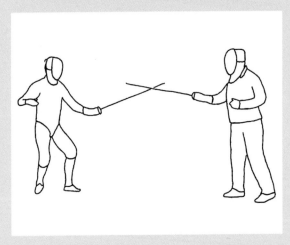

ABOVE: Fig. 119   The pupil engages the blade...

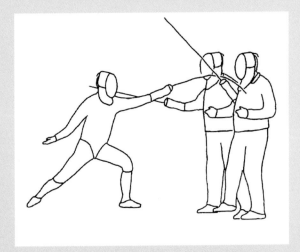

RIGHT: Fig. 120   ...and launches an attack.

The secret is to get 100 per cent success and do it very slowly.

2. Next, the coach introduces a fast parry and riposte from quarte (*see* Figs 121–122).

   a This can be a direct riposte.

   b. Or, a riposte with disengagement (indirect), If there is an answering pressure on the blade.

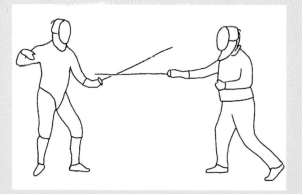

Fig. 121   The coach introduces a fast parry of quarte...

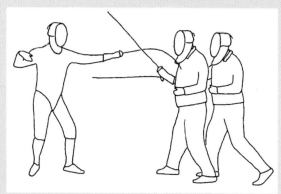

Fig. 122   ...and riposte.

The coach does this with different timings: hesitating, going in fast, starting from different blade positions. The reason for the change of pace is that the pupil must look for the coach's blade. The variations listed in this lesson are a reservoir of ideas, to be used sparingly.

   Now combine 1 and 2. The ultimate aim is to provide choice reaction on all these variations.

3. The pupil steps forward, with feint of a straight thrust. On the coach's response, he does the appropriate variation (*see* Figs 123–124).

   a. Disengagement to high-line, deceiving a simple parry.

   b. Drop to low-line (target selection). The coach covers high, slightly lifting the sword hand.

   c. Counter-disengage if there is a circular parry.

Fig. 123   The pupil steps forward with a feint of straight thrust...

Fig.124   ...and attacks with the appropriate variation.

It would be tempting to refer to the last action as a doublé. Strictly speaking a doublé is a feint of disengagement, followed by a counter-disengagement. Starting with a feint of a straight thrust is almost, but not quite, the same thing. Much of the time, fencers prefer the guard of sixte with no blade contact and so present a simple feint without changing line.

   Combine 1, 2 and 3.

117

4. After 3, the pupil returns to sixte, does a parry of circular sixte and ripostes (*see* Figs 125–126)

a. This is done very fast and direct. If the coach moves in close, the riposte might be performed with opposition.
b. If the coach applies pressure to the blade, the riposte may be with disengagement (indirect).
c. If the circular parry is deceived, the pupil does a fast successive parry of quarte, then riposte.

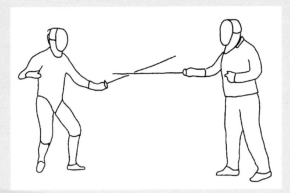

ABOVE: Fig. 125   The pupil parries circular sixte...

RIGHT: Fig. 126   ...and ripostes.

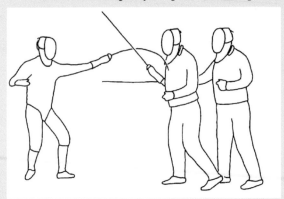

Combine 1, 2, 3 and 4.

Next, to slow the fight down and take control, the following is applied:

5. The pupil straightens his arm, with the point in line. As the coach goes for the blade, he performs a dérobement (*see* Figs 127–128).

a. If the coach goes slowly for the blade, the pupil does dérobement.
b. If the coach goes quickly for the blade twice, the pupil does double dérobement.
c. If, after a successful dérobement, the coach does a beat attack, the pupil does parry and riposte. Against a good beat attack, a successful dérobement may not be possible, in which case the pupil reverts immediately to parry and riposte.

Fig. 127   The pupil presents the point in line...

Fig. 128   ...then does a dérobement.

If your opponent does not go for the blade after the straight arm is presented, this is fine because you will still have regained control of the fight and slowed him down.

Combine 1, 2, 3, 4 and 5.

Having slowed down the fight successfully, you may want to speed it up again.

6. The coach moves his blade a little forward. The pupil launches a sudden beat attack (*see* Figs 129–130).

a. The pupil chases the coach down the piste when the coach lifts the blade; then does a beat attack with lunge.

b. If there is a fast reaction by the coach, the pupil does a beat attack with disengagement.

Fig. 129   The pupil launches a sudden...

Fig. 130   ...beat attack.

Make sure the pupil finds the blade. Do a clean beat attack that is instantly recognizable to a referee. Combine 1, 2, 3, 4, 5 and 6.

7. The coach walks forward with a very slow attack; the pupil has to take a different parry and riposte each time this action comes around in the lesson (*see* Figs 131–133).

a. In a fighting situation your opponent is seeing this parry for the first time, hence a different parry each time. The aim is to produce a winning hit.

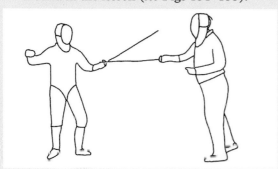

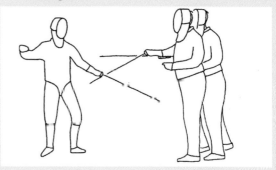

ABOVE: Fig. 131   The coach walks forward with the point extended.

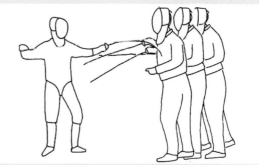

ABOVE RIGHT: Fig. 132   The pupil must take a new parry each time...

RIGHT: Fig. 133   ...and riposte successfully.

You have to keep your distance if you wish to take a different parry each time. Your opponent, on the other hand, does not want you to keep distance. This is where I instinctively parried quarte against Bert's slow walking attack and got a firm telling-off for selecting a parry that had already been used earlier in the lesson. Next time around, I parried raised sixte, missed on the riposte and got another telling-off. I redeemed myself on the next cycle, with an octave parry, taken against a high-line attack, riposting with opposition – but got myself into trouble again for repeating octave (a favourite) on the next cycle. To be successful in this requires a little pre-planning. For example, wait in octave, then parry sixte; wait in quarte, then parry circular quarte; use prime; use septime; etc.

Combine 1, 2, 3, 4, 5, 6 and 7.

A reaction parry and riposte can be added to any of these, at any time in the lesson. This is very much a fighting lesson and should last about thirty minutes, moving all the time.

The same theory applies to sabre and épée, but with different strokes.

Platform of Seven Sabre Actions

The coach moves backward and forward throughout this lesson, ensuring that the pupil is constantly on the move and keeping correct sabre distance. Some of these moves are very slow in order to build up reactions and open eyes awareness, which will be done over the course of several lessons.

The main core actions and optional variations might be as follows:

Main Core of Actions

1. The coach holds the blade horizontally, across his target, lifting the blade up or down, giving a fighting opening. He may then proceed to introduce a counter-riposte, remise or redoublement.

Variations

a. The pupil goes for head or flank. The coach gradually reduces the size of these openings, causing the pupil to speed up.

b. The coach introduces a counter-riposte from the pupil. To a quinte parry of the head cut, he may initiate a counter-riposte of quarte–head or tierce–head while the fencer is still on the lunge. A flank cut may be parried by the coach in seconde, with a counter-riposte by the pupil of tierce–head. Depending on the coach's presentation of the blade, other parries and counter-ripostes may be employed.

c. Next is a remise or redoublement. The coach parries quinte, then lowers the blade momentarily, hesitating with the riposte. The pupil suddenly remises to head. On the pupil's attack to flank the coach parries seconde, again pausing briefly. The fencer does a very fast redoublement, with cut to top of wrist. Both renewals can be followed by tierce riposte head.

The remise or redoublement initiates a sudden change of pace. The counter-ripostes, by contrast, are taught very slowly. As always, the coach may substitute any other actions that seem appropriate.

Next, parries and ripostes may be introduced.

120

2. The coach attacks to chest or flank

   a. The pupil parries quarte or tierce, with riposte direct to head.

   b. The parry of quarte may be taken with a step back and a lunge with riposte to flank. The locations of the pupil's hits will vary, depending on the coach's final blade positions.

As always the variations are used sparingly.

Combine 1 and 2.

The core work here is very simple. There may be a short delay between 1 and 2, perhaps a long delay, or none at all.

3. On the coach's opening, the pupil does head–flank.

   a. The coach's opening begins in quarte.

   b. The coach's opening begins in tierce.

   c. The coach's opening begins in quinte. (The pupil waits until the hand drops.)

The key element when going compound is to open up the distance. Throughout this lesson, continue to open up the sabre measure, with increasing mobility. If the student messes up, always start from the beginning.

Bert pointed out that my cut to flank was a horizontal – not the classical angulated cut, with rising cut from below the guard. The classical cut to flank can revert to wrist if the opponent steps back. It also forces the opponent to parry seconde, which opens up flank–right cheek, –head, –left cheek and –chest cut.

Combine 1, 2 and 3.

4. After 3, the pupil returns to guard and then does tierce, riposte head, or successive parries, or a stop-cut.

   a. The parry of tierce, riposte to head, is done very fast and direct.

   b. For successive parries, the pupil parries quarte, then a fast tierce, riposte head. This could also be parry of quinte, then a fast seconde, riposte head, etc.

   c. If the coach initiates a compound attack on the pupil's return to guard, this will often provoke a stop-cut by the pupil. Against the coach's chest–flank attack, the pupil parries quinte, stop cut to wrist, then parries tierce riposte head. Against the coach's head–flank attack, the pupil parries quinte, stop-cut to top of wrist from the quinte hand position, then parries high seconde, with riposte to head. The initial parry of quinte is not a 'feint' of a parry, because the pupil, at this point, genuinely believes that the coach's attack to head is genuine.

The addition of a sudden riposte of tierce-head, introduced by the coach on the pupil's return to guard, ensures that the pupil is covered. So many people go back on guard lazily.

Combine 1, 2, 3 and 4.

Next, to slow the fight down and take control, the following is applied:

5. The pupil straightens his sword arm, with the point in line. As the coach goes for the blade, he performs a dérobement.

   a. If the coach goes slowly for the blade, the pupil does dérobement.

   b. If the coach goes quickly for the blade, twice, the pupil does double dérobement. A typical Hungarian sabre lesson might involve several compound dérobements.

   c. If the coach beats the blade (many fencers will hesitate when doing this), the pupil does stop-cut to wrist immediately. A step back or parry may also be added.

In an actual fight situation, a fencer may wish to return to guard with the arm extended and in line after the head–flank, in order to offer the point in line (omitting 4).

Combine 1, 2, 3, 4 and 5.

Having slowed down the fight successfully, you may wish to speed it up again.

6. The pupil threatens a cut to head. On the coach's presentation of the blade, the pupil does a, b or c.

   a. The pupil accelerates with a very fast beat attack.

   b. The pupil does stop-cut to arm, stepping back if required.

   c. The pupil does a fast attack to arm, on the coach's preparation.

Combine 1, 2, 3, 4, 5 and 6.

7. The coach walks forward with a very slow attack. The defender has to take a different parry and riposte each time this action comes around in the lesson.

   a. This is a ludicrously slow attack. The pupil must change defence, or change the line of the riposte. The aim is to produce a winning hit.

Combine 1, 2, 3, 4, 5, 6 and 7.

At this point, I responded much better than my attempts at foil, perhaps because this is my stronger weapon. This lesson is simpler than at foil, but varying distance is very important.

Platform of Seven Épée Actions

The main emphasis in this épée lesson is on remise and redoublement. As before, the coach moves backward and forward throughout this lesson, ensuring that the pupil is constantly on the move and keeping correct épée distance.

The main core actions and optional variations might be as follows:

Main Core of Actions

Variations

1. The coach walks backward and forwards at épée fencing measure, occasionally offering a wrist opening: top, right, left and below the guard.

   a. The pupil lunges to the wrist openings.

   b. The pupil lunges to the wrist openings, the blade is parried; on release of the blade, the pupil does remise.

c. The pupil lunges to the wrist openings, the blade is parried; on release of the blade, the pupil does remise; on the return pressure on the blade by the coach, the pupil does redoublement with disengagement.

d. The pupil lunges to the wrist openings, the blade is parried and held onto briefly by the coach, anticipating remise; the pupil does disengagement, with redoublement to arm.

e. The pupil lunges to the wrist openings, the blade is parried; as the coach steps forward, the pupil does disengagement, with redoublement to arm, on the return to guard. (At foil your first instinct might be to parry and counter-riposte. When going back to guard, the épéeist still adopts an offensive attitude; in épée the point is the first line of defence.)

f. The pupil lunges to the wrist openings, the blade is parried; the pupil does disengagement, as the coach steps backward with redoublement to arm, using a forward reprise.

The coach does not move too fast, so that the fencer gets 90 per cent-plus of the hits correct. The pupil has to respond to the correct opening to wrist, 'open eyes'. The remaining remise or redoublement options are 'choice reaction'.

Next, circular sixte:

2. The coach presents his blade for a circular sixte riposte.

   a. If the coach's hand is high, the pupil does riposte with disengage or prise-de-fer, circular sixte bind to septime, finishing with hit to leg or foot.

   b. If the coach's hand is low, the pupil does a time-thrust through circular sixte, with hit to arm.

The height of the coach's hand gets the required reaction, followed by target selection.

Combine 1 and 2.

3. The coach either leaves his blade still or goes for the pupil's blade. The coach will defend with circular sixte.

   a. If the coach's blade is temporarily still, the pupil picks it up on the sixte side, followed by a disengagement, and counter-disengagement (doublé) – a creative action.

   b. If the coach goes for the blade, the pupil does disengagement, and counter-disengagement (doublé) – an opportunistic action.

123

This should be done at varying distances, with a variety of footwork.

Combine 1, 2 and 3.

On the return to guard, generally, the coach can spend a lot of time altering the position of the pupil's hand. For example:

	Variations	**Notes**
On the return to guard the pupil can…	a. Leave the sword arm straight, making a classic hit on the arm as the coach moves forward.	i. This can lead to dérobement, or double dérobement, if the coach goes for the blade.
		ii. Or, if the coach takes the blade successfully, a ceding or opposition parry can be used.
		iii. If the coach beats the blade, the pupil can stop-hit to wrist (often with angulation), following the beat, according to how the blade is presented.
	b. Draw the sword hand back very quickly to the épée on guard position. (This fast withdrawal could also be to tierce or octave.)	i. Because the pupil withdraws the sword hand quickly, this is intended to confuse the opponent on distance, straightening his arm prematurely. The pupil immediately rotates through circular sixte, instantly straightening his arm. This has exceedingly fast arm and point speed, making it very effective on someone rushing in. This fast counter-attack changes the speed of the phrase.
		ii. If the coach keeps moving forward, finish to body.
	c. Lay the point under the coach's sword hand in the 5 or 6 o'clock position, on the guard. This ensures that the return to guard is in an offensive position (not purely defensive). This is an exercise in knowing where the point is and how it affects the phrase which follows.	i. The pupil stop-hits to underside of wrist, as the coach moves forward. The coach cannot beat the blade or take prise-de-fer with the point in this position.
		ii. The pupil can do redoublement using circular sixte, with opposition, to top of the arm. The tactic of putting the point under the guard may draw the opponent into dropping the guard to cover, making the top of the arm vulnerable.
		iii. With the point under the hand, if attacked the pupil can take sixte, tierce, quarte, seconde or octave (even prime, if the hand is well forward).
		iv. The blade angle here is shallow and not easy to take, but there is always someone willing to try. If the coach attempts to take the blade, the pupil does dérobement to top arm.
		v. If the coach attempts to take the blade and hesitates, the coach does immediate redoublement to knee or foot.

Next, a beat attack is introduced.

4. The coach lifts his blade

a. The pupil beats the blade on the quarte side, then lunges with hit to arm.

b. If the coach's foot moves forward at the same time, the hit will land on the body.

This épée beat is done turning the hand and using the edge of the blade. Because you are beating on the quarte side, the opponent's point should end up next to the rear leg. The pupil gets to know where the point should end up (*see* Figs 134–136). A beat at épée that leaves the point up is of little value, unless you are going for counter-time. Beating the blade heavily (once or twice), followed by beating the blade lightly near the guard with the top end of the blade, finishing on the wrist, is unique to épée (*see* Figs 137–139). In foil and sabre, striking the lower third of the opponent's blade would be deemed a parry. The success of this action stems from the lack of priority in épée.

Fig. 134 This épée beat is done turning the hand...

Fig. 135 ...using the side of the blade, placing the opponent's point next to the rear leg...

Fig. 136 ...finishing on the wrist.

Fig. 137 Beating the blade heavily...

Fig. 138 ...then lightly, near the guard...

Fig. 139 ...finishing on the wrist.

Combine 1, 2, 3 and 4.

Now start by introducing a simple or compound attack, to leg or foot.

5. The coach gives an opening to outside arm. The pupil lunges to outside arm.

    a. If parried, the pupil does immediate redoublement to leg.
    b. If the coach does not parry, the pupil completes the compound attack: arm–leg.

    Or, the coach gives no opening.

    c. If there is no opening, the pupil steps forward, feints to mask, then attacks to foot.

    Or, the coach straightens his sword arm.

    d. The pupil does prise-de-fer attack to leg.

    Or, on the coach's opening, the pupil steps forward, straightening to inside wrist.

    e. On coach's response of circular sixte, the pupil does a counter-disengagement and lunge to body.
    f. If coach steps back, the hit reverts to wrist.
    g. This time, as coach steps back, the pupil counter-disengages, takes the blade and lunges with opposition to arm.
    h. As for g, but if coach lifts his hand, the pupil places his point under the coach's sword hand, with pronation, and immediately hits to foot. The use of pronation like this will often get an opponent to withdraw his hand back a little.

Always do these compound attacks with a change of speed: start slower, accelerate after the deception. As you finish the attack, you may wish to consider pronating the sword hand; the hit can end up under the wrist or on the leg.

Combine 1, 2, 3, 4 and 5.

Next is prise-de-fer. Near the end of a fight a 'jabbing match' can develop. For the purpose of this exercise, we will just use envelopment. The correct condition for prise-de-fer is when the opponent's arm is straight, with the blade moving forward – otherwise you may lose contact with the blade and leave yourself susceptible to redoublement.

6. The coach begins by placing the blade on the top of the pupil's guard; the pupil takes circular sixte.

    a. The pupil moves the sword hand a little back, then takes the riposte with opposition.
    b. The pupil moves the sword hand a little forward, then does envelopment. In the context of this lesson, this may end up with a lunge or flèche. To get either hit, the pupil must move

fairly quickly. If the pupil's hand moves too far back, he can be caught under the hand. If the blade moves too far forward, he will not be able to envelop.

c. If the blade slips clear, while the coach's arm is still extended, the pupil does double prise-de-fer, taking the blade in quarte, finishing in the low-line. If the attempt to take the blade in quarte is deceived, the pupil takes sixte envelopment.

d. The coach takes an opposition parry of sixte or tierce. The pupil does redoublement to body. A fencer's weight can be on the back foot when taking an opposition parry, opening up the lower target for hits to knee or foot. These options, leaning back or not leaning back, could be used as target selection in a lesson on its own.

The coach lifts his blade.

e. The pupil beats the blade on the quarte side. The coach counter-attacks to inside wrist, off the beat. The pupil does circular sixte envelopment. (Many épée coaches teach counter-attacks off the beat, catching the foilist, who is used to having priority.)

The coach gives an opening to arm. The pupil lunges to arm and is parried.

f. The pupil returns to guard, leaving the point in the 5 or 6 o'clock position. As the coach moves forward, he stop-hits under the arm, then takes sixte envelopment.

Combine 1, 2, 3, 4, 5 and 6.

7. The coach walks forward with a very slow attack; the defender has to take a different parry and riposte each time this action comes around in the lesson.

a. Various responses may be considered. Although circular sixte has already been used, you can parry sixte then, if deceived, use circular sixte. Quarte can be used, with riposte in opposition, or quarte croisé to leg. Raised sixte is higher than at foil, taking the opponent's point clear of the mask, allowing a riposte to the top of mask, holding onto the blade. Starting on the sixte side, take septime (which can be lifted to raised septime); the riposte here is with detachment.

At the end, each riposte should be made covered so that there is only one light at the end of the fight. Your opponent will have had plenty of time to work out what your favourite stroke is. If you take a parry that he has not seen before, you will have the advantage.

   Combine 1, 2, 3, 4, 5, 6 and 7.

   These lessons should be built up gradually over a period of time. To start with, make simple lessons out of each part, then combine them, 1, 2, 3, etc. As you get to know your pupil, begin to elaborate and develop one section at a time per lesson.

Knowledge of tactics will create top-flight fenc-ers. Height, age, speed and whether the fencer is left- or right-handed must all be taken into consideration, but this is the art of coaching. Giving a thirty-minute lesson on tactics will keep the coach refreshed.

Having looked at many different types of indi-vidual lessons, we will consider how to demon-strate to a class.

Demonstrating to a Class

When coaches take exams, involving a variety of different fencing movements, they can easily forget what they are trying to present. As in maths, we should try to remember a simple formula and build the presentation around it.

Consider this example of stepping forward and backward. A simple movement – or is it?

1. Find another name for it. Many books refer to gaining and breaking ground.
2. **Why** do we do it? We gain ground to get into a position where we can score a hit. Breaking ground is the greatest defence in the world. If the opponent cannot reach you, you cannot be hit. Because this is something you do in order to get into a position to score, this comes under the **definition** of a 'preparation'.
3. The **technique** can be described as follows: stepping forward, heel-toe (front foot), toe-heel (rear foot); stepping backward, toe-heel (rear foot), heel-toe (front foot). Four basic movements.
4. If, however, we reduce this to three move-ments, we can reduce the **timing** on step-ping forward, heel-toe (front foot), and as the toe goes down we simply move the rear foot forward in a single movement. Some world-class masters lift the heel and allow the rear toe only to land, providing more spring in the lunge on stepping backward, toe-heel (rear foot), as the heel goes down we simply move the front foot back in one action.
5. Make a game for two fencers, one stepping forward and backward, the other keeping distance. As the fencers begin to speed up (especially beginners), they will tend to be off **balance**. Your body weight should always be distributed evenly between the feet when stepping forward and backward. When you are moving easily and with elegance, you will feel less tired.
6. If both fencers keep perfect distance, no one will hit. The attacker may step back slowly and then step forward suddenly, as the opponent advances, in order to gain the initiative. Alter-natively, he may bring his rear foot forward to touch his front heel in order to gain 18 inches (450mm) on his first step.

Why–Definition–Technique–Timing–Balance

Give a beautiful demonstration of the subject you want to teach. Then fill in around the outline of these key words.

5   Additional Techniques

Some additional topics arose quite naturally during various lessons and discussions at Wallace Fencing Club. These follow, in no particular order, beginning with the now widespread use of the orthopaedic foil grip.

The Orthopaedic Foil Grip
Initially the black plastic Leon Paul orthopaedic foil grip was introduced into British fencing. Some masters concluded that it would harm classical fencing technique, since it would spoil finger play.

Bert had used a French grip for eighteen years, but it was when fencing in the 1974 World Professional Championships in Karlsruhe that the foil grip kept being taken out of his hand. He went to the armoury at lunch time, had a couple of foils changed to orthopaedic grips and was more successful in the afternoon.

At a fencing club in Paris, Bert observed a French fencing master teaching a whole class the correct use of the orthopaedic grip. The master explained the 'ripple effect' by holding both hands on the floor, manipulating his fingers,

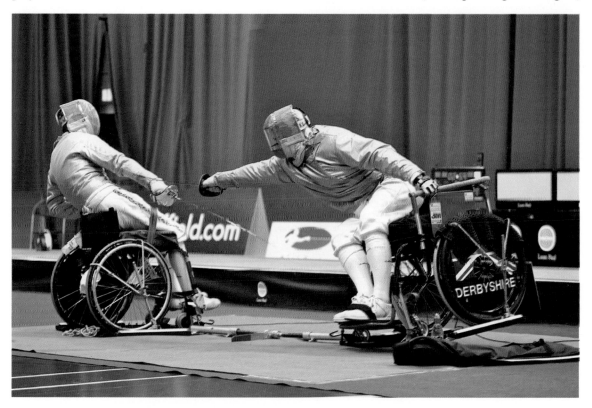

Fig. 140   Men's Sabre, British Wheelchair Fencing Championships, 2010. (Photo: Graham Morrison)

Fig. 141 The little finger pulls the blade in line.

Fig. 142 The second finger supports this; the blade is now in line.

Fig. 143   The third finger also pulls the blade in line and holds it there...

Fig. 144   ...leaving the thumb and forefinger free to steer the blade.

lifting each in turn, each following the last, making a rippling, almost wave-like motion like a pianist. He demonstrated how most fencers snatch the orthopaedic grip with all four fingers. He made the fencers fetch the blade in line using only the little finger, then place in the remaining three fingers from the bottom up. The little finger pulls the blade in line; the second finger supports this, and the blade is now in line. The third finger also supports the blade in line and holds it there, leaving the thumb and forefinger free to steer the blade, acting as 'manipulators' – as described in Roger Crosnier's *Fencing with the Foil* (*see* Figs 141–144). The foil may now be manipulated as if using a French grip.

Coaching with an orthopaedic foil grip for extended periods can cause problems. With many, the upper flange presses into the upper palm, in the centre just below the fingers, which has a debilitating effect, in time leading to more wristy movements. If this flange is machined out, it can be used like a French grip, with no more ensuing problems (*see* Fig. 145).

What is the correct size for an orthopaedic grip? The bottom part of the 'handle' should be level with the base of the palm. If the grip is too small (higher than this), it will dig into the hand.

Using a Training Wall Chart

At Wallace Fencing Club, Bert uses training wall charts, based on the Scottish Schools Grading System (*see* Fig. 146). Bert first introduced these training routines in 1971 when he was Scottish National Fencing Coach: they currently consist of six levels per weapon, each containing twelve training routines. Different coloured badges and certificates are awarded for each level. The names of the fencers are inserted on the left-hand side. Twelve tasks are listed along the top of each chart; after completing each task successfully, the relevant box is ticked by the coach.

With this system, a young person can see his progress. Any that fall behind can catch up. A coach, using this system, can devise individual lessons that are more responsive. Fencers may be introduced to new weapons relatively quickly. Those who do not elect to fence competitively still have skills targets to aim for.

The same training charts can be used in wheel-chair fencing, if you leave out the footwork. In

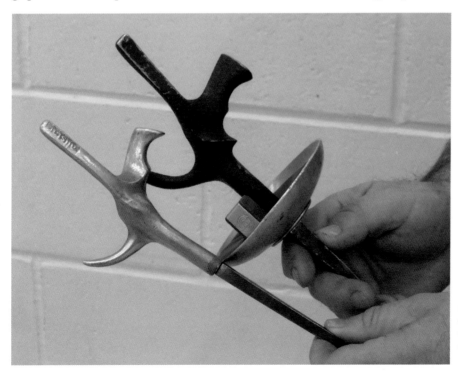

Fig. 145 The orthopaedic foil grip – a standard grip (above), the flange removed (below).

FOIL ONE

NAME	THE GRIP	ON GUARD	STEPS FORWARD AND BACKWARD	LUNGE AND RECOVERY	THE HIT	STRAIGHT THRUST	DISENGAGE FROM SIXTE AND QUARTE	STEP AND LUNGE WITH DISENGAGE AND CUTOVER	PARRY SIXTE AND QUARTE	ADD RIPOSTE TO 9.	PARRY SIXTE, PARRY QUARTE-RIPOSTE	PARRY AND LUNGE WITH DISENGAGE RIPOSTE
	1	2	3	4	5	6	7	8	9	10	11	12

NOTES: (A) WHEN ATTACKING WITH A LUNGE WHEN SHOULD THE FRONT FOOT LAND? (B) WHAT IS THE PRINCIPLE OF DEFENCE? (C) HOW IS THE HIT MADE?

Fig. 146 Scottish Schools Grades – Foil One.

1970, Bob Anderson had proposed adapting the AFA's Proficiency Awards so that candidates might take lessons, or fence, from a wheelchair. For those interested in coaching, the British Disabled Fencing Association has produced a DVD, *Wheelchair Fencing Coaching – Foil and Sabre*, featuring Prof. Laszlo Jakab.

Bert worked at Lothian Fencing Club at Cameron House in Edinburgh for many years, where wheelchair and able-bodied fencers competed together in the same club. One remark-able individual was John Clark, a wheelchair fencer who became a World and Paralympic champion, and showed how to overcome adversity.

Placing the Point on an Extended Horizontal Finger

The coach's left hand is presented at chest height with the index finger horizontal, at right angles to his partially extended arm. The pupil then straightens his sword arm, resting the last inch (25mm) of the blade on the coach's finger. The coach presses the pupil's point off his finger, either using his foil or gloved hand, allowing the pupil to do a disengagement, then replacing the point, carefully using the fingers, until resting once again on the coach's horizontal finger. This is an effective routine for helping to improve point control.

For the purposes of these exercises, the coach's finger may be presented at three different heights: chest height, chin height and next to the low-level target.

Another way is to do the same training routine with the pupil in the half lunge position.

These days, practising point control may be achieved using an electronic hit selection device, practising hits at straight arm distance, half lunge

and full lunge distance. The object is to hit one of five points on an electronic score board. With this system the coach stands to one side. Each pupil should do ten perfect hits, then the times can be compared; penalty time deductions may be added for misses. Various programmes may be selected to simulate remise, or redoublement scenarios, etc.

Bert demonstrated how you could stand on guard, making minor adjustments to your on guard position, to see which would produce the fastest results. You are unlikely to get any real benefit from a training apparatus like this unless you are always standing on guard correctly.

The importance of correct balance in the on guard position cannot be overstressed. While watching a girl fencing in a club competition, Bert pointed out that she was leaning forward and was attacking with steps forward rather than lunging, because it was so difficult for her to lunge from this position.

Bert went on to simulate a training routine, similar to the hit selection device, using the horizontal index finger on his left hand: moving to each of the five positions shown on the board and getting the pupil to do one-two, doublé, low-high, one-two-three, doublé dégagé, etc.

Stepping Forward

Although we were primarily thinking about foil when we had this discussion, these principles might well apply to other weapons.

If you step forward with the rear foot flat on the ground, it can be difficult to reverse direction. Moving the rear foot forward onto the ball of the foot, with the heel clear of the ground, makes it easier to reverse; when attacking, by the time the heel hits the ground, the arm is straight (*see* Figs 147–149). The defender is vulnerable when the attacker's point passes the opponent's guard. The attacker needs speed to finish: dropping the heel, straightening the rear leg at the same time, delivers this. There is a natural reaction for the

Fig. 147 Stepping forward...

Fig. 148 ...onto the ball of the foot...

step heavily on the heel tend to wobble a little as they move forward, which may be noticed by the referee.

Stepping Forward and Backward
As the front foot moves forward, the rear foot moves back, almost with the same timing. The opponent is trained to attack when the fencer moves his front foot, perhaps with a beat attack on the preparation. The front foot recedes,

defender, when faced with a point accelerating at close quarters, to parry quarte, opening the way for a fairly devastating one-two attack.

Stepping forward, with the rear heel lifted, is more solid. Bert demonstrated this by getting me to apply sideways pressure to his unarmed shoulder. With his heel down, it was easier to push him off balance; when raised, the natural spring in his foot offered more resistance. Fencers who

Fig. 149 ...then dropping the heel, straightening the rear leg at the same time, delivers speed.

allowing sufficient distance to easily parry and riposte. There is little that the attacker can do to respond to this as he gets caught inside his own reaction time.

Fencers are taught to react to distance. An advanced fencer will begin to launch his attack a fraction ahead of the opponent's step forward.

As the front foot moves back, the rear foot moves forward, almost with the same timing. The opponent steps forward, believing the fencer is stepping back, only to be caught with a short, fast lunge.

Lunging with a Different Timing

The following lunge was taught to Bert by a leading French coach.

Start by kicking the front leg forward. The sword arm will be straight, by the time the front foot reaches the ground (*see* Figs 150–151). This has a peculiar timing, since the sword hand overtakes the front foot. The emphasis here is on the terrific speed of the straightening arm and acceleration of the point.

Zbigniew Borysiuk, in *Modern Saber Fencing*, refers to this technique as an 'accelerating lunge', where the attacker begins by thrusting out the front foot, the sword hand held back, preparing for an explosive finish and taking the opponent by surprise. The opponent may parry too early by responding to the front foot, effectively trying to parry something that is not yet there. The attacker carries out a deception by only doing a straight thrust (feinting with the foot).

Care must be taken when using this technique, as referees may conclude that the attacker (at foil) does not have right of way, since the arm is not

Fig. 150 Start by kicking the front foot forward.

Fig. 151 The sword arm will be straight by the time the front foot reaches the ground.

extended at the outset and the attacker may be susceptible to a counter-attack (*see* Fig. 152).

Left-Handed Fencer

Bert took lessons where he was required to turn the toe of his rear foot in, which had the effect of moving the sword hand over, allowing it to naturally compensate for a left-hander (*see* Fig. 153). This helped to cover against a straight thrust, against a coulé down the blade, and ensures that

the right-hander does not react to an open target on the sixte side, leaving him vulnerable to attack in the low-line.

Fig. 152 The attacker may be susceptible to a counter-attack.

Fig. 153   Turn the toe of the rear foot in, which moves the sword hand over.

Fig. 154 This is how people used to fence sabre.

at a moment's notice from here. This can be compared to an athlete's reaction to the start of a sprint race (*see* Figs. 154–158). When the gun is fired in a sprint race there is a slight delay before the athlete begins to run. A stationary fencer will also experience a slight delay before launching an attack.

Notes on Bert Giving a Sabre Lesson
I was watching Bert give a sabre lesson in the club, and he did a few things that I had not seen

Fig. 155 The fencer moves his hand...

W. M. Zaaloff in *The Foil Fencer's Pocket Book* advises against attacking left handed fencers on the quarte side. However, a parry of quarte and riposte by disengagement, or cutover, can be effective.

Never Sit On Guard with the Hand Still
Sometimes a sabreur can move his hand up and down – from quinte, the blade horizontal, keeping the sabre moving. Attacks can be launched

Fig. 156   ...keeping the sabre moving.

Fig. 157   Attacks can be launched at a moment's notice...

him do before. The pupil was in the on guard position. Bert feinted into the front of the blade, then asked the pupil to take circular quarte from this position, sometimes called cutting-the-line. Moving in close, he taught the pupil to riposte at speed, from tierce and quarte, with back cuts (*see* Figs 159–160). As many advanced sabreurs do not respond to feints, he taught a compound attack of head–flank in the middle of a phrase. On the coach's lunge to head (short), the pupil was taught to beat upwards with hit to head, avoiding side-to-side actions that are easier to predict.

A fencer who returns to guard with the sword turned a little, lowering the point from tierce, makes it more difficult for the opponent to launch a beat attack. If this is attempted, he may disengage and cut to wrist – a typical response – perhaps drawing parry of tierce, riposte head, or even circular quarte, riposte to head. A defender who pauses in quarte may stop-cut from this position, using the angle, then parry tierce, riposte head. For stop-cut, parry-riposte, keep your steps back at the same length; if you vary the length of the steps, it is difficult to get the distance right.

Fencing Notation

Keeping a written record of fencing lessons or training routines is helpful, whether it is the teachings of great masters or insights gleaned from working with more experienced fencers. Most of this book was written in note form on the floor during fencing lessons while still wearing a fencing glove. Luckily I was able to decipher my scrawl after the event.

Terence Kingston in *Epee Combat Manual* describes his fencing notation system: essentially a form of fencing 'shorthand', which allows notes to be taken very quickly. Julio Martinez Castello in *The Theory and Practice of Fencing* and John Smith in *Foil Fencing: The Techniques and Tactics of Modern Foil Fencing* refer simply to Fencer A and Fencer B, ascribing actions or positions to each. Although a more 'longhand' approach, to the uninitiated it is easy to follow.

In the following example of a sabre training session, I have used the Fencer A/Fencer B approach, starting first at sabre fencing measure. Fencer A begins each sequence; fencer B responds appropriately. At the end of each session, sabre fencing measure is resumed. Some explanatory notes are added.

Fig. 158   ...like an athlete's reaction to the start of a sprint race.

Fig. 159   A back cut riposte at close quarters.

Fig. 160   Another back cut riposte at close quarters.

An Example Sabre Training Session

Start at step and lunge distance for a cut to head or body.

Fencer A	**Fencer B**
1. Moves the blade from any defensive position to another.	In the on guard position. Steps forward and lunges with a cut to head, or body.

Fencer A
- Offering an open or opening line.

Fencer B
- The arm extension is completed with the landing of the rear foot.
- The hand is rotated neatly (if required) to adopt the final line.
- The cut is executed lightly with the fingers.

Recovers backward with sword arm still straight. Steps backward and then resumes the on guard position.

- The fencers are once again at step and lunge distance for a cut to head or body.
- The on guard position may now be safely resumed.

Fencer B is now successfully attacking various parts of the sabre target. Fencer A now has a reason to introduce a parry-riposte. The riposte should immediately follow the meeting of the blades.

Fencer A	**Fencer B**
2. Moves the blade from any defensive position to another.	In the on guard position. Steps forward and lunges with a cut to head or body. Stays on the lunge.

Fencer A
- Offering an open or opening line.

Does appropriate parry-riposte. Resumes the on guard position.

Fencer B

Recovers backward with sword arm still straight. Steps backward and then resumes the on guard position.

- The fencers are once again at step and lunge distance for a cut to head or body.

Next, we introduce an alternative way of returning to step and lunge distance for a cut to head or body.

Fencer A	**Fencer B**
3. Moves the blade from any defensive position to another.	In the on guard position. Steps forward and lunges with a cut to head or body. Stays on the lunge.

Fencer A
- Offering an open or opening line.

Does appropriate parry-riposte. Immediately steps backward, after the hit lands. Resumes the on guard position.

Recovers backward with sword arm still straight and then resumes the on guard position.

- The fencers are once again at step and lunge distance for a cut to head or body.

Now Fencer A closes distance at the start, allowing Fencer B to attack with a lunge into the preparation.

4. Moves the blade from any defensive position to another and steps forward.

   - Offering an open or opening line.
   - The fencers are now at lunge distance for a cut to head or body.

In the on guard position. Lunges with a cut to head or body. Stays on the lunge.

Does appropriate parry-riposte.

Resumes the on guard position.

Recovers backward with sword arm still straight, steps backward and then resumes the on guard position.

- The fencers are once again at step and lunge distance for a cut to head or body.

In the next routine, Fencer B must be careful not to launch the attack until Fencer A has ceased moving backward.

5. In any defensive position. Steps backward (pauses).

In the on guard position. Steps forward, in response.

- The step should not be too large as the opponent may wish to launch an attack into the preparation.
- The fencers are once again at step and lunge distance for a cut to head or body.

Moves the blade from initial defensive position to another.

- Offering an open or opening line.

Steps and lunges (explosively), with cut to head or body. Stays on the lunge.

Does appropriate parry-riposte. Resumes the on guard position.

Recovers backward with sword arm still straight, steps backward and then resumes the on guard position.

- The fencers are once again at step and lunge distance for a cut to head or body.

In the above exercise, Fencer A occasionally omits the parry-riposte, to see if Fencer B's cuts will land true.

Next, we introduce a counter-riposte to the sequence.

6. Moves the blade from any defensive position to another.

- Offering an open or opening line.

  Parries with a small step backward and begins to riposte.

- The small step backward is taken to improve the effectiveness of the parry against the deep attack.

- Stepping backward may cause a slight delay between the parry and riposte.

- This small delay allows Fencer B to recover backward.

  Lunges with the riposte.

  Recovers backward with sword arm still straight, steps backward and then resumes the on guard position.

- The fencers are once again at step and lunge distance for a cut to head or body.

In the on guard position. Steps forward and lunges deeply with a cut to head or body. Stays on the lunge.

Recovers backward with sword arm still straight.

Parries and counter-ripostes.

- The parry is taken from the straight arm position, with the sword arm well forward.

Resumes the on guard position

At step and lunge distance for a cut to head or body, Fencer B's first step may draw an attack into the preparation.

7. Moves the blade from any defensive position to another.

- Offering an open or opening line.

  Lunges into the preparation with cut to head or body.

  Recovers backward with sword arm still straight and then resumes the on guard position.

- The fencers are once again at step and lunge distance for a cut to head or body.

In the on guard position. Takes a small step forward, as if beginning an attack.

- The fencers are now at lunge distance for a cut to head or body.

Steps back immediately, still in the on guard position.

- Fencer A's attack is short.

This time, Fencer A has to be a little faster off the mark, if Fencer B is to be caught on the preparation.

8. Moves the blade from any defensive position to another.	In the on guard position. Begins to step forward, moving the front foot.
• Offering an open or opening line.	
Lunges into the preparation with cut to head or body.	Completes a short step forward; with the landing of the rear foot does parry-riposte.
• Reacting to the movement of the front foot.	• This is second intention.
Recovers backward with sword arm still straight and then resumes the on guard position.	Steps backward with the arm still straight and resumes the on guard position.
	• The fencers are once again at step and lunge distance for a cut to head or body.

All the above can be practised with increasing mobility. Steps can be performed at varying lengths and speeds. Sudden changes in direction can often be a good precursor to launching an attack.

Whatever form of notation you chose, recording what you learn or observe should lead to improved performance and increased enjoyment.

A Few Short Maxims

The following is taken from George Roland's *A Treatise on the Theory and Practice of the Art of Fencing*, some of which may still be of use to young fencers today:

A few Short Maxims which the Young Fencer will do well to Keep in his Recollection.

1. Always place yourself on Guard out of the possible reach of your opponent's Longe.
2. When you present the foils, give the choice without pressing.
3. Neither appear to exult at giving thrusts, nor show ill temper at receiving them.
4. If you are much inferior, make no long assaults.
5. Make no movement without considering its probable consequences.
6. If the eye and wrist precede the foot, the execution will be just.
7. Avoid making all uncertain and dangerous attacks.
8. If you can hit without a feint, make none; two motions being more dangerous than one.
9. Be not angry at receiving a hit, but by keeping your temper, endeavour to convert your present loss to your future improvement.
10. Before you applaud a thrust, examine if it be not effected by accident.
11. Endeavour to discover your adversary's designs, and to conceal your own.
12. Although your position be firm and vigorous, they cannot be correct unless they accord with those of your opponent.
13. A good fencer fights more with the head than the hand.
14. Twenty good qualities will not make a perfect fencer; one fault prevents your being so.
15. Judge of a thrust by reason rather than from its success.
16. To know what you may risk, you must know what you are worth.

Roland's thoughts were published in 1823, but an almost identical list appears in Ramon Castellote's *The Handbook of Fencing* in 1882.

In Conclusion

I met up with Bert at Wallace Fencing Club. There was a competition that day, so I found him alone, sitting near the entrance in one corner of the empty gym, doing his paperwork; he said there were too many distractions at home. We talked together for an hour or so, as old friends do.

He wanted to remember a training routine he had experienced with some Dutch coaches, early in his career. Apparently there were twelve parts to it, which he tried to recall:

1. It starts with a number of foils laid out, evenly spaced in a straight line on the floor. The trainee fencers step forward in the on guard position, without their feet touching the foils, then return stepping backward. This is timed. A second is added each time a foot touches a foil. On completion, they will touch the next person to go. Gradually we build up precision. Foils evenly spaced on the floor allows for repetition, gradually improving until a rhythm develops and the fencers can step at full speed against the clock.

2. Next, some of the foils are placed closer together and others further apart, randomly. The fencers then proceed, timed as before. Observation and memory come into play. This is harder. Each time a foot touches a foil a second is added. The journey forward and backward is no longer predictable. Greater concentration is required and there is a greater chance of error, particularly on the return journey, when the fencers are trying to remember where the foils are.

3. Now the foils are placed in a circle and again the fencers have to step between the foils without touching. This is timed, but this time if a fencer knocks a foil it has to be put

back, which takes extra time, adding additional pressure. The fencers are no longer moving in a linear fashion. The distance to be traversed tapers between the foils, so that if a fencer strays from the centre, the distance will become longer or shorter, requiring immediate correction. The first three exercises have become progressively more difficult. Now a change of pace is introduced.

4. A foil is placed across the back of the fencer's neck, with either end held under the arms. The fencer rotates side to side, from the waist. The foil exaggerates these rotations, making the exercise more beneficial.

5. The foil is held vertically, by the blade, with the sword arm extended. Using only the fingers, the foil is manipulated up and down, lifting the blade upwards being the more difficult of the two – excellent for developing finger play.

6. The foil can be balanced on the point, on either hand, and made to stand up. To be successful and to maintain balance, the fencers must keep their feet moving at all times, which is very tiring on the legs. Also, they must wear masks at all times to protect their faces.

7. The fencers stand with their legs spread out and pass the foil in a figure of eight, around and between their legs. This is done ten times. If they touch a leg, it has to be done another ten times. You will appreciate that in going from exercise to exercise, the fencers are becoming progressively more tired. Arms that are tired may find it difficult to complete this exercise properly, leading to forced errors and further repetitions, continuously building up the pressure.

8. Next is a wonderful game. The fencers stand

in a circle, each holding a foil with the palm on the pommel and point on the floor. The coach calls 'left' or 'right' and everyone in the circle responds, releasing their own foils and reaching for their neighbours' without letting them drop. Invariably some will start in the wrong direction and correct. Others will let the foil fall to the floor. Eventually all will succeed and the whole unit responds as required. Needless to say, this learning process can have hilarious consequences.

9. Half the fencers sit in a circle on the floor, with the foils extended to the outside, occasionally raising a foil. The training fencers must step over the foils, in the on guard position, or pause and jump over if the foil is lifted. The fencers who have been resting on the floor swap with those who have been active, allowing them also a brief respite.

10. The fencers face each other in pairs. One holds a foil horizontally by the blade, in both hands, and drops it. The other must catch it with both hands. The secret is to bend the knees quickly. Fencers can observe others successfully catching the foil and copy their technique. It is best to do this exercise on a training mat, to avoid damaging the floor; or alternatively the guards may be removed from the foils.

11. Do a flèche over three foils, or a balestra, or step and lunge by moving the positions of the foils, holding a foil in your sword hand at the same time so that it feels a part of you. This can be made as hard as you like. Footwork can be mastered individually, perhaps working to correct a particular weakness, or progressively in different combinations, pushing individuals' endurance and ability to the limits.

12. Lastly, the foils are placed in a long ladder on the floor, similar to the first exercise. Jump two, pick up the third, or any other sequence ordered by the coach. When you get to the end of the line, do the same exercise in reverse, returning the foils to their previous locations. You begin the return journey with a lot of foils. Relocating them, while carrying a load, requires great fitness

and dexterity. Done conscientiously, you should have pushed yourself completely on all twelve exercises.

Actually, Bert remembered all twelve parts. When Bert coaches, he is usually quite animated. Today he seemed more pensive. After finishing, he said he had nothing left to teach me. He had spoken this way before, but had always returned after a break refreshed, with something new. This time, apparently, he meant it. Thus concluded our discussions at Wallace Fencing Club.

We have come so far. Each of these advanced fencing techniques has been learned individually, studying only one stroke at a time before proceeding to the next. At the time, each was hard enough to learn and often completely new to me. Looking back, I have particular favourites. One was learning the Italian guard at foil. Bert had taken many lessons in his early years with an Italian foil. Here, he with his orthopaedic handle and I with my French handle took great pleasure is demonstrating how he could dominate the blade by disarming me again and again, sending my foil flying down the gym, which I dutifully retrieved. His simple delivery of the hit at épée, on the wrist, was remarkable, and the demonstration of the unique sabre grip, taught to him by Alf Simmonds, memorable.

These come from a time when the tradition of fencing required an understanding of technique, a willingness to explore, and a mastery of swordsmanship stemming from historical traditions. I have a second-hand copy of F.C. Reynolds' *The Book of the Foil*, in which the author has handwritten a dedication: 'May courage and courtesy ever attend your blade' (1935). To me this says it all.

Many of the ideas in this book were right for their times. The advanced fencer is an amorphous individual, whose techniques may be taken from the past, resulting from changes in the rules or types of equipment – or from sheer serendipity, following an inspired hunch. Fencers and coaches will always do what they believe in. Believing in something is perhaps halfway to making it work.

Feel free to accept, or reject; but at least understand why.

About Bert Bracewell

Bert started fencing aged seventeen, after seeing the film *Scaramouche* (released 1952) at the Rialto, South Woodford. When leaving the cinema, he saw a small postcard advertising a fencing club called 'Latista'. He went along and soon felt at home. There, he met Prof. Alf Simmonds, from whom he discovered a love of classical fencing, which he still has today.

At eighteen, he started National Service, becoming an armourer at RAF Kirkham. He was the only fencer there, but a Physical Training instructor took him in hand and he competed regularly. He recalls being told: 'You've got a superb attack, but no defence!'

After completing his training, he was posted to RAF Water-beach (outside Cambridge), where the Commanding Officer, Group Captain Chacksfield, was president of the RAF Fencing Union. The station adjutant was captain of the fencing club. They fenced most weeks, in matches against universities, etc., and were never beaten. 'Groupie', as the Commanding Officer was known, wished that this operational station could win the RAF Team Championships – which

they did, in the second year. Bert's introduction to épée, being a foilist and sabreur, was when Physical Training instructor André Williams, a Frenchman and superb fencer, told him he

Fig. 161 Bert Bracewell (left) and Laszlo Jakab (right).

would be entered in the Fighter Command Épée Competition. On asking advice, he was told: (1) keep your point on the target; (2) if the other attacks, straighten your arm and run; and (3) after you have attacked, do redoublement and hope. He came third and won Fighter Command Colours.

On leaving the RAF, Bert returned to Latista, which had now moved to Marylebone, London, fencing there for a couple of years. He became Secretary of the club and ran three Leaders courses. On taking the training exam he passed top in foil and épée and second in sabre. He was advised by Dame Mary Glen-Haig, Charles de Beaumont and Bob Anderson to consider becoming a coach, which he ignored. He ran the club for three months, also fencing every weekend. Suddenly finding himself ill in hospital with throat ulcers, it became obvious that he could not maintain this lifestyle. At the same time, he was asked to join an Olympic training squad and was engaged to be married. He decided to marry and coach properly, if he could, taking lessons from and observing many fine coaches. He formed his own club, Cyrano, which produced the first British World Under-20s finalist, and was one of the few people from that time to understand singlestick.

Singlestick is a game which can be thought of as the cutting equivalent of the épée. The whole body is target. The Royal Navy had used the singlestick as a substitute for the cutlass (which was not withdrawn from service until 1936) for safer, realistic, free play. The stick is made from a 40-inch (1m) length of Mountain Ash, running through a basket or hide leather hilt. The use of the point is considered dangerous and is counted as a hit against the defender. Like épée, the aim is to hit without being hit. Unlike modern fencing, players may circle and use the terrain. As with épée, ripostes with opposition remove the possibility of remise or redoublement. Each man was honour-bound to acknowledge his opponent's hits; if there was no cry of 'Touche', no hit was scored. A great enthusiast of singlestick was the late Colonel Hay, who wrote a pamphlet explaining its rules and conventions. He did a lot of singlestick at Gibraltar and helped to formulate the rules set forth in the pamphlet. The rules for both cudgel and singlestick were developed between the wars by the Gibraltar garrison and naval establishment, and are known as the Calpe, which is the classical name for Gibraltar. I met Colonel Hay in Edinburgh in the late 1960s and he gave me a copy of his pamphlet, which I kept for many years. The Colonel took épée lessons from Bert Bracewell into his eighties.

Just before the last exam for his master's diploma, Bert was asked to try for the job of Scottish National Coach. Johnny Fethers, the then Maître d'Armes to SAFU, who was returning to Australia in 1964 to coach their Olympic fencing team, had recommended him. SAFU appointed Bert as the first National Coach, by arrangement with the Scottish Education Department, and he proceeded to build up fencing in Scotland to a high standard. He said: 'Being National Coach is a great job, but you must be able to remove the knives from your back, regularly.' He came north in 1966 and became a full Professor in 1967.

Tommy Hope's introduction in the SAFU newsletter read:

> …Members have yet another reason to be grateful to Maître John Fethers… Before leaving Scotland he put the Committee in touch with one who has now been chosen to succeed him, and who has been appointed National Fencing Coach for Scotland as from 1 August 1966. The National Coach is Herbert Thomas Bracewell, aged thirty… In the British Professional Championships, Mr Bracewell has been runner-up to Maître Fethers four times…and he (Bert) was Sabre representative of the BAF (British Academy of Fencing) at the World Professional Championships in Stuttgart.

Bert fought in the World Professional Championships a total of five times, at all weapons.

His enthusiasm, skill and persistence over nearly two decades were recognized in 1980, when the BAF awarded him the Gauthier Trophy. He retired from Scottish Fencing after twenty-six productive years, becoming a lecturer in stage combat at the Royal Scottish Academy of

Music and Drama, Glasgow and Queen Margaret University, Edinburgh. Now he coaches a few keen fencers and will help any coach training for a BAF of Fencing qualification.

Any master can make a good coach, but only exposure to other masters makes a master. Bert has suggested the names of key figures in his development as a fencing master.

- Prof. Bob Anderson: for an understanding of the problems of being a national coach and the work ethic required for the job.
- Prof. Alf Simmonds: for love of the sport and a desire to do things correctly and clinically.
- Prof. Steve Boston: for the business side of fencing.
- Prof. Reggie Behmber: how to be a gentleman coach.
- Prof. Bill Harmer-Brown: who always gave a professional lesson, even when tired.
- Provost Bill Jones: who taught Bert so much about the épée; an unsung hero.
- Prof. Norman Miller: the best physical trainer and friend.
- Prof. Gomar Williams: who worked with Bert on their masters diplomas.
- Maître Johnny Fethers: who recommended Bert for the job of Scottish National Coach.

Postscript

The Children and Families Department of the City of Edinburgh Council have granted permission for the following article and photograph to be published. It is taken from *Dolphin*, the school magazine of Ainslie Park Secondary School, 1968:

Fencing

Thanks to the enthusiasm of the National Fencing Coach, Professor H.T. Bracewell, the standard of fencing in the school has improved considerably. In the Scottish competitions our pupils distinguished themselves, the girls' team winning the team event, and Mary Telford, Jacqueline Watt, Moira Wood and Jackie Wood gaining places in the Scottish Schoolgirls.

Robert Jamieson and Edward Rogers were third and fourth in the Scottish Schoolboys, and Edward Rogers was sixth in the Junior Sabre, which is an open competition. Following on these successes, five of our club were chosen to fence for Scotland against Northern Ireland and Eire: Edward Rogers, vice-captain of the team, with foil and sabre; Robert Jamieson, foil; Stewart Dodds, sabre; Peter Charleston, épée; Mary Telford, foil. And they won, congratulations!

Our junior members are showing great promise, and we hope for great things from them in the future.

The year is 1968. The clock on the school gym wall approaches 2pm. Our busy Friday lunchtime training session with Bert is over. Mr McLachlan is telling us to put away the fencing kit in the large storage cupboard outside, off the corridor. We can see the schoolyard through the wooden wall bars, where children are gathering; afternoon lessons await. The sky is overcast. A thin mist of rain falls into the grey playground below, punctuated by occasional bursts of colour from school uniforms. It is the autumn term; the fencing season has just started. Full of expectations, we are already thinking of the weekend and our next competition.

Bert has just left the gym…

Fig. 162
(*Back row, left to right*) R. Bird, P. Charleston, A. Bird; (*middle row*) G. Hansen, S. Dodds; (*front row*) E. Rogers, J. Wood, C. Malcolm, J. Meader, J. Pinkney, R. Jamieson. (Photo: City of Edinburgh Council)

Glossary

À temps perdu loss of fencing time

Area of indecision a zone between the high- and low-lines where the distinction between parrying high or low is unclear

Beat-parry a parry administered by a sharp beat

Choice reaction (1) a logical response to more than one stimulus

Choice reaction (2) Bert's definition is 'off the blade' as opposed to 'open eyes' where the blade is not found

Circular parry where the point of the blade is thought to travel in a full circle, also most effective when the point describes an ellipse

Combination parries successive parries (Alaux)

Compound parries successive parries (Wyrick)

Compound preparations two or more preparations taken simultaneously

Compound prises-de-fer two or more prises-de-fer taken continuously without losing contact with the opponent's blade

Composed attacks compound attacks

Composed parries successive parries

Cone of defence a cone on its side which includes the blade movements of an épée

when the point is retained in the same position and the guard is moved from side to side and up and down to deflect the opponent's attacks to the wrist

Conscious timing is the tempo chosen when the opponent is in some kind of motion (Vince)

Continuity hitting a rhythm exercise involving continuous hits which helps to instil confidence in a fencer's technique

Contraction parry similar to a circular parry but taken in the opposite direction at the same time travelling across to the opposite line

Corresponding parry a parry taken from high-line to low or low-line to high on the same side (Gravé)

Coulé a graze down the opponent's blade, executed by straightening the arm and keeping contact with the blade throughout

Counter-parry see circular parry

Counter-time provoking an offensive or counter-offensive reaction so that it can be opposed with a riposte or an attack

Coupé dessous feint of cutover deceiving a simple parry by disengagement into the low-line, often carried out as one continuous action, rolling the hand into pronation

Cutting-the-line see contraction parry and diagonal parry

153

Diagonal parry a parry taken diagonally across the target from high- to low-line or vice versa

Double preparations two preparations taken successively

Double prises-de-fer two or more prises-de-fer during which there is a momentary loss of the blade

Doublé a feint of disengagement drawing a circular parry, which is then deceived by counter-disengagement

Doublé de doublé a feint of a doublé followed immediately by another doublé in the opposite direction

Doublé dégagé a doublé followed by disengagement

Flick-hit a hit delivered in cutover fashion, exploiting the momentum gained from the weighted point of a modern foil or épée

Flying cutover to attack or riposte by means of a combined beat and backward glide along the opposing blade, followed instantly by the cutover

Foible the weak part of the blade from the centre to the point

Forte the strong part of the blade from the centre to the guard

Froissement this displaces the opponent's blade by means of a sharp strong grazing action forward and downwards from foible to forte

Gaining measure bringing the rear foot forward close to the front foot to approach an attack

Holding parry holding the incoming blade briefly but firmly in the exact position after contact has been established (Nadi)

Inquartata an evasive manoeuvre executed by pivoting the front foot and moving the rear foot sideways, making a half turn to the outside line to avoid being hit

Jury the referee and judges who officiate at a fencing event

Modern disengage attack a form of broken-time compound attack (Simonian)

Neuvième sometimes called the ninth position of the blade or raised sixte

Open eyes (1) starting a movement with no prior knowledge of how it will finish, relying on reflexes to adjust and make the correct ending

Open eyes (2) Bert's definition is 'where the blade is not found', which he does to differentiate between this and choice reaction

Pointe d'arrêt a 'biting' point on an épée which allows hits to land

Raised sixte *see* neuvième

Remise (1) a renewal of the attack in which the blade remains in the line in which it was parried

Remise (2) Bert's definition at foil includes an angulated continuation with a small forward shoulder movement

Remise (3) Bert's definition at sabre includes renewals in a different line about the wrist

Remise attacks are attack actions that immediately follow a previously unsuccessful attack riposte or counter-attack (*The Complete Guide to Fencing*)

Sentiment du fer the feel in the opponent's blade through contact of the blades

Sesta the parry of sixte at sabre

Singlestick a game, which can be thought of as the cutting equivalent of the épée

Slinging parry *see* tap parry (Barbasetti)

Spanking parry essentially a beat-parry (Nadi)

Steam a slang term which refers to traditional pre-electric fencing with judges

Subconscious timing where the moment to launch an attack is suggested by instinct (Vince)

Successive parries two or more parries taken against a compound attack or counter-attack

Tac parry essentially a beat-parry (Tau)

Tap parry essentially a beat-parry (Barbasetti)

Bibliography

Alaux, M., *Modern Fencing: Foil, Épée, and Sabre* (Charles Scribner's Sons, New York, 1975)

Amateur Fencing Association, *Fencing (Foil, Épée, Sabre)* (Educational Productions Ltd, 1957)

Amateur Fencing Association, *Fencing* (A. and C. Black (Publishers) Ltd, 1994)

L'Amie, N., St C., 'Enter Bert' (*The Point*, Issue 35, May 1993)

Anderson, B., *Improve your Fencing* (Wolfe Publishing Ltd, 1970)

Anderson, B., *All About Fencing* (Stanley Paul and Co. Ltd, London, 1970)

Anderson, B., *Better Fencing – Foil* (Kaye and Ward, London, 1973)

Barbasetti, L., *The Art of the Foil* (Hutchinson and Co. Ltd, London, 1933)

Barth, B., Beck, E. (Eds) *The Complete Guide to Fencing* (Meyer and Meyer Sport (UK) Ltd, 2007)

de Beaumont, C-L. (Ed.) with Crosnier, R., *Fencing Technique in Pictures* (Hulton Press, London, 1955)

de Beaumont, C-L., *Fencing: Ancient Art and Modern Sport* (Nicholas Kaye, London, 1960)

de Beaumont, C-L., *Fencing* (The English Universities Press Ltd, 1968)

de Beaumont, C-L., *Your Book of Fencing* (Faber and Faber Ltd, London, 1970)

de Beaumont, C-L., *All About Fencing* (Coles Publishing Co. Ltd, Toronto, 1978)

Behmber, R.H., *Fencing* (Arco Publications, London, 1965)

Beke, Z., and Polgár, J., *The Methodology of Sabre Fencing* (Corvina Press, Budapest, 1963)

Bertrand, L., *The Fencer's Companion* (Gale and Polden Ltd, 1948)

Borysiuk, Z., *Modern Saber Fencing* (SKA Swordplay Books, 2009)

Bower, M., *Foil Fencing* (McGraw-Hill Higher Education, 1997)

Bracewell, H., T., *Advanced Foil Coaching* (1976)

Campos, J., *The Art of Fencing: Three Weapons, Foil, Épée, Sabre* (Vantage Press, New York, 1988)

Castello, J.M., *The Theory and Practice of Fencing* (Charles Scribner's Sons, 1933)

Castellote, R., *The Handbook of Fencing* (Ward, Lock and Co., London, 1882)

Castle, E., *Schools and Master of Fence* (Arms and Armour Press, 1969)

Cheris, E., *Fencing: Steps to Success* (Human Kinetics, Publishers Inc., 2002)

Cohen, R., Book Review – 'Sabre Fencing, by D. F. Evered' (*The Sword*, October 1982)

Cohen, R., *By the Sword* (Macmillan, 2002)

Collings, T.A., *Classic Foil Fencing* (Terence A. Collings, 2003)

Crosnier, R., *Fencing with the Sabre* (Faber and Faber Ltd, London, nd)

Crosnier, R., *Fencing with the Épée* (Faber and Faber Ltd, London, 1958)

Crosnier, R., *Fencing with the Electric Foil* (Faber and Faber Ltd, London, 1961)

Crosnier, R., *Fencing with the Foil* (Faber and Faber Ltd, London, 1967)

Cross, T., and Kirkham, E., *Introduction to Fencing* (Stipes Publishing L.L.C., 1996)

Curry, N.L., *Fencing* (Goodyear Publishing Company Inc., 1969)

Curry, N.L., *The Fencing Book* (Leisure Press, New York, 1984)

Deladrier, C., *A Comprehensive Manual for the Foil, the Épée, the Sabre* (Paladin Press, 1948)

Dunn, H.A.C., *Fencing* (G. Bell and Sons Ltd, London, 1911)

Evangelista, N., *The Art and Science of Fencing* (McGraw Hill, 1996)

Evered, D.F., *Sabre Fencing* (Gerald Duckworth and Co. Ltd, London, 1982)

Evered, D.F., 'Pre-Electric Épée Judging' (*The Sword*, July 2010)

Fleck, J.M.M., 'Obituary – Colonel Robert Alastair Hay R.E. 1897–1984' (*The Sword*, July 1985)

Garret, M.R., *Fencing* (Bailey Brothers and Swinfen Ltd, Folkestone, 1971)

Garret, M.R., and Poulson, M.H., with Sobel, S., *Foil Fencing Skills, Safety Operations, and Responsibilities for the 1980s* (The Pennsylvania State University Press, 1981)

Garret, M.R., Kaidanov, E.G., Pezza, G.A., *Foil, Saber, and Épée Fencing: Skills, Safety, Operations, and Responsibilities* (The Pennsylvania State University Press, 1999)

Gaugler, W.M., *A Dictionary of Universally Used Fencing Terminology* (Laureate Press, Bangor Maine, 1997)

Gaugler, W.M., *The Science of Fencing* (Laureate Press, Bangor, Maine, 1997)

Gravé, F., *Fencing Comprehensive* (Hutchinson and Co. Ltd, London, 1934)

Gray, E., *Modern British Fencing 1964–1981* (Amateur Fencing Association, 1984)

Harmenberg, J., with Ceci, R., Pingree, G. and Väggö, B., *Epee 2.0: The Birth of the New Fencing Paradigm* (SKA Swordplay Books, 2007)

Hett, G.V., *Fencing* (Sir Isaac Pitman and Sons Ltd, London, 1951)

Hill, L., Bruce, P. and Combes, I., *Professor Bob Anderson 1922–2012* (British Academy of Fencing, 2012)

Kingston, T., *Epee Combat Manual* (Terence Kingston, 2001)

Lidstone, R.A., *The Art of Fencing: A Practical Manual for the Foil, Épée and Sabre* (H.F. and G. Witherby, London, 1930)

Lidstone, R.A., *Fencing: A Practical Treatise on Foil, Épée and Sabre* (H.F and G. Witherby Ltd, London, 1952)

Lukovich, I., *Electric Foil Fencing* (Corvina Press, 1971)

Lukovich, I., *Fencing: The Modern International Style* (SKA Swordplay Books, New York, 1998)

MacDonald, E. and I., *The Art of Fencing* (W. Foulsham and Co. Ltd, London, 1938)

Madden, L., Lt Cmder, 'Cudgels and Singlestick' (*The Sword*, July 1986)

Manley, A., *Complete Fencing* (Robert Hale Ltd, 1979)

McGrath, J., Barton, M., *Naval Cutlass Exercise* (Royal Navy Amateur Fencing Association, 2002)

Morton, E.D., *Martini A–Z of Fencing* (Queen Anne Press, 1988)

Nadi, A., *On Fencing* (Laureate Press, Bangor, Maine, 1994)

Nelson, M., with Reiff, R., *Winning Fencing* (Henry Regnery Company, Chicago, 1975)

Nobbs, P.E., *Fencing Tactics* (Philip Allan, London, 1936)

Norcross, T., *Fencing: The Foil* (Ward Lock, Ltd, 1978)

Paul, S., Miller, W., Beasley, P., Bottoms, L., with Usher, G., *Épée Fencing: A Step-by-Step Guide to Achieving Olympic Gold* (Wellard Publishing, 2011)

Pitman, B., *Techniques of Foil, Épée and Sabre* (The Crowood Press Ltd, 1988)

Reynolds, F.C., *The Book of the Foil* (Ernest Benn Ltd, 1931)

Roberts, L.E., *Notes on Foil Fencing* (1936)

Rogers, E., 'Single-Stick: The Calpe Methods and Rules' (*The Point*, Issue 64, July 2001)

Rogers, E., 'Sabre Fencing' (*The Point*, Issue 65, July 2001)

Roland, G., *A Treatise on the Theory and Practice of the Art of Fencing* (Archd. Constable and Co., Edinburgh, 1823)

Shaff, J., *Fencing* (Atheneum, New York, 1982)

de Silva, H., *Fencing: The Skills of the Game* (The Crowood Press Ltd, 1991)

Simmonds, A.T., and Morton, E.D., *Start Fencing* (The Sportsman's Press, London, 1989)

Simmonds, A.T., and Morton, E.D., *Fencing to Win* (The Sportsman's Press, London, 1994)

Simonian, C., *Fencing Fundamentals* (Charles E. Merrill Publishing Company, 1968)

Simonian, C., *Basic Foil Fencing* (Kendall/Hunt Publishing Company, 1995)

Simonian, C., *Get the Point! A Fencer's Handbook* (Kendall/Hunt Publishing Company, 2006)

Sise, P., *A Basic Foil Companion* (SKA Swordplay Books, 2010)

Skipp, A., *Handbook of Foil Fencing* (Coachwise Ltd, 1999)

Skipp, A., *Handbook of Epee and Sabre* (Coachwise Ltd, 2010)

Slade, S., *Fencing for Fun!* (Compass Point Books, 2009)

Sowerby, A., *Fencing; Skills, Tactics, Training* (The Crowood Press Ltd, 2011)

Smith, J., *Foil Fencing: The Techniques and Tactics of Modern Foil Fencing* (Summersdale Publishers Ltd, 2003)

Standing Sub-Committee for Technique and Terminology, *Summary of Fencing Theory and Terminology* (British Academy of Fencing, January 2002)

Stocks, R., *The Art of Foil Fencing* (Sway Fencing Club, 2007)

Szabó, L., *Fencing and the Master* (SKA Swordplay Books, 1997)

Tau, B.H., *Fencing Volume One, Competitive Training and Practice* (Wysteria Publishing, New York, 2005)

Tau, B.H., *Fencing Volume Two, The Foil* (Wysteria Publishing, New York, 2006)

Tau, B.H., *Fencing Volume Three, The Épée* (Wysteria Publishing, New York, 2006)

Tau, B.H., *Fencing Volume Four, The Sabre* (Wysteria Publishing, New York, 2006)

Vass, I., *Epee Fencing: A Complete System* (SKA Swordplay Books, 1998)

Vince, J., *Fencing* (A.S. Barnes and Co. Inc., 1940)

Volkmann, R., *Magnum Libre d'Escrime* (1997)

Wojciechowski, Z., *Theory, Methods and Exercises in Fencing* (Amateur Fencing Association)

Wyrick, W., *Foil Fencing* (W. B. Saunders Company, 1971)

Zaaloff, W.M., *The Foil Fencer's Pocket Book* (W. M. Zaaloff, 1949)

Index